FRIEDRICH NIETZSCHE'S
THIRD UNTIMELY MEDITATION
SCHOPENHAUER AS EDUCATOR

Translated with Notes by Daniel Pellerin

To Richard and Jon

Contents

Foreword

In his later years, Nietzsche grew so fond of posing as a latter-day Thor, instructing the modern world on how to philosophize with a sledgehammer, at least when he felt the camera-eyes of posterity upon him, that one might be surprised at how gently he once used a chisel and a brush to sculpt a portrait of his idol from ancient marble. Elsewhere we might hear Nietzsche thundering about the need to sacrifice meaningless millions to the worthy few, but in his homage to Schopenhauer, made to personify Nietzsche's own ideas about education in the most comprehensive sense, we see him starting from a different premise altogether, namely the singular marvel that is every human being, every one entirely unique, every one thrown together from such curiously multifarious ingredients into the single thing that he is, once and once only.

The strict logic of his uniqueness, Nietzsche writes, makes man beautiful and remarkable, novel and incredible like all works of nature, and certainly not boring. If men so often look contemptible, it is because they allow themselves, out of laziness and fear, to degenerate into mere factory products. Yet any human being who wishes to be more than a herd animal need only stop making things easy for himself. Let him follow the call to be himself, to shed what is false about him, to become a little mischievous and rid himself of the shackles of opinion and fear, to consider what his soul has truly loved instead of merely killing time, and everything changes. It is by helping us make such a turn that true educators do us such an invaluable service. But they can only point the way: "No one can build you the bridge on which you, and only you, must cross the river of life. There may be countless trails and bridges and demigods who would gladly carry you across; but only at the price of pawning and forgoing yourself. There is one path in the world that none can walk but you. Where does it lead? Don't ask, walk!"

A NOTE ON THE TRANSLATION

THE PAGE BREAKS IN BRACES REFER TO THE TEXT IN THE *Kritische Studienausgabe* {KSA} edited by Giorgio Colli and Mazzino Montinari (Munich: DTV, 1999), pp. 335-427. All references to the KSA are by volume and page number, and all translations not otherwise attributed are my own. For *Thus Spoke Zarathustra*, I am using Walter Kaufmann's translation (Penguin, 1978), cited by book and page number.

A Note on the Text

Between 1873 and 1876, Nietzsche published four rather disparate essays, of which this one was the third, under the common heading of *Unzeitgemäße Betrachtungen*. The term *Meditations* (for *Betrachtungen*) suggests itself in English not only because of its fitting dictionary meaning ("serious and sustained reflection or mental contemplation" [OED]), but also because another set of famous musings, those of Marcus Aurelius, would have been known to Nietzsche under the German title *Selbstbetrachtungen*.

Nietzsche repeatedly stresses how *unzeitgemäß* (lit. not in accordance with time) he considered himself to be. Thus in the Preface to the Second of his *Meditations*: "Only insofar as I am a sapling (or pupil: *Zögling*, sharing a common root with *Erziehung*) of more ancient times, especially the Greek, have I arrived at such untimely experiences of myself in these times" (*Vom Nutzen und Nachteil der Historie für das Leben*: KSA 1.247). Beyond insisting that his thought is "out-of-season," as some translations would have it, Nietzsche challenges the limitations of a time-bound perspective in general, most clearly in paragraphs 22 {362} and 31 {374} below. As he writes in his unfinished manuscript on "Philosophy in the Tragic Age of the Greeks" (ca. 1873): "It lies in the nature of great philosophical men that they must disregard all that is merely current and momentary." (PtZG, section 8: 1.833-34)

Although Nietzsche dedicated his essay to the memory of Schopenhauer, the title is rather misleading. In *Ecce Homo*, at the end of his productive life, when he is "looking back from a distance" upon his writings, Nietzsche concedes: "I do not wish to deny that at bottom they speak only of me... In 'Schopenhauer as Educator,' it is my innermost history, my own *becoming* that is inscribed... Really it is not 'Schopenhauer as Educator' who speaks here, but his *opposite*, 'Nietzsche as Educator.'" (KSA 6.320) The idea that even the greatest educator could relieve one of the burdens of *self-education* is revealed as youthful folly in par. 6 {341-42}. "No one can build that bridge for you" (par. 3 {340}).

That said, Schopenhauer did see himself, along the very lines imagined by Nietzsche, as one of "the great spirits ... [who are] the real educators of the human species, ... born into the world so that they may steer men towards the truth on the ocean of their errors and to raise them up, towards the light, towards culture, towards refinement, out of the dark abyss of their crudity and vulgarity." (*Aphorismen zur Lebensweisheit*, edited by Franco Volpi [Stuttgart: Kröner, 2007], ch. 5, p. 186).

Friedrich Nietzsche's
Third Untimely Meditation (1874)
Schopenhauer as Educator

I

[1] THAT TRAVELER WHO, HAVING SEEN MANY LANDS AND PEOPLES and continents, was asked what human trait he had kept finding everywhere, replied: "They tend to be lazy." One might object that it would have been more accurate and valid for him to say: "They are all timid." They hide behind customs and opinions. At bottom every human being understands very well that he is entirely unique on this earth and that not even the strangest coincidence will ever again throw together such curiously multifarious ingredients into the single thing that he is; he knows, yet he hides it like a guilty conscience — but why? Because he fears his neighbor, who demands conventional behavior and disguises himself with it. But what forces an individual to fear his neighbor, to think with the herd, and to take no joy in himself? Modesty, perhaps, in a couple of rare cases. In most cases by far, it is a matter of comfort, inertia, in short, the very tendency towards laziness mentioned by the traveler. He is right: human beings are even more lazy than they are timid, and what they fear most of all are the troubles with which an unconditional honesty and bareness would burden them. Only the artists despise this casual compliance with borrowed manners and cloak-like opinions and reveal the secret cause of everyone's

1

guilty conscience, namely that every human being is a singular {337-38} marvel;[1] they dare to show us man being himself down to the subtlest twitch of his muscles, himself alone, and what is more, they show that the strict logic of his uniqueness makes him beautiful and remarkable, novel and incredible like all works of nature, and certainly not boring. If great thinkers despise mankind, it is on account of man's laziness: for thus do they look mass-produced, irrelevant, unworthy of being engaged or improved. Any human being who does not wish to be part of the masses need only stop making things easy for himself. Let him follow his conscience, which calls out to him: "Be yourself![2] All that you are now doing, thinking, desiring, all that is not you."

[2] Every young soul hears this call by day and by night and shudders with excitement at the premonition of that degree of happiness which eternities have prepared for those who will give thought to their true liberation. There is no way to help any soul attain this happiness, however, so long as it remains shackled with the chains of opinion and fear. And how hopeless and meaningless life can become without such a liberation! There is no drearier, sorrier creature in nature than the man who has evaded his own genius and who squints now towards the right, now towards the left, now backwards, now in any direction whatever. Such a man becomes, in the end, unfit for any kind of handling, for he is no more than a hull without a core, a tattered, gaudy, pompous scarecrow, a specious specter that cannot arouse even fear, let alone commiseration. And if it is fair to say of the lazy man that he is killing time, then one must also be seriously worried that a period relying for its well-being on public opinion, that is, on private laziness, will one day really be killed: I mean that it will be erased from the recorded history of life's true liberation. How very distasteful it must be for later generations to concern themselves with the legacy of such a period, in which it was not living men who did the ruling, but publicly opinionating pretenders.[3] {338-39}

Hence our age may well turn out, in the estimation of some remote posterity, to be the darkest and most obscure part of history,[4] because it is the least human. When I walk along the new streets of our cities, I think to myself that of all these horrid houses raised by the tribe of public opinionaters, nothing will remain in a hundred years, and that by then the opinions of these builders will likewise have fallen to pieces. What hopes, by contrast, may be cherished by all who do not feel themselves citizens of this age; for if they were its citizens, they, too, would be contributing to the killing of their age and would perish with it — whereas they are striving instead to revive these times and to keep on living themselves.

[3] But even if the future left us nothing to hope for — our peculiar existence in this very Now should be the greatest encouragement to us for living by our own measure and law. That is, we should take heart from the inexplicable fact that we happen to live precisely today, even if it took us all eternity to arise; that we possess nothing more than an arm's-length of Today, in which we should demonstrate why and for what end we happened to arise just now. We must give a responsible account of our existence before our own selves; it follows that we must wish to be real helmsmen of this life rather than allowing it to become thoughtless and arbitrary. One must take a somewhat mischievous and dangerous attitude towards existence, especially since one will always lose it in the end, however poorly or well things may turn out. Why cling to a miserable patch of land, or a particular profession? Why listen to one's neighbor's chatter? How petty it is to bind oneself to views that lose their power to oblige a few hundred miles down the road. East and West are chalk-marks drawn to mock our timidity. Let me try to find my way to freedom, the young soul says to itself; and is it to be deterred because two nations happen to hate and fight each other, or because there happens to be an ocean separating two continents, or because somewhere a religion happens to be in currency that {**339/340**} did not exist

even a few thousand years ago? "None of that is really you," says the soul to itself. "No one can build you the bridge on which you, and only you, must cross the river of life.[5] There may be countless trails and bridges and demigods who would gladly carry you across; but only at the price of pawning and forgoing yourself.[6] There is one path in the world that none can walk but you. Where does it lead? Don't ask, walk!"[7] Who was it that spoke these words: "No one rises so high as he who knows not whither he is going?"[8]

[4a] But how do we find ourselves again? How can man know himself? It is a dark, mysterious business: if a hare has seven skins, a man may skin himself seventy times seven times without being able to say, "Now that is truly you; that is no longer your outside." It is also an agonizing, hazardous undertaking thus to dig into oneself, to climb down roughly and directly into the tunnels of one's being.[9] How easy it is thereby to give oneself such injuries as no doctor can heal. Moreover, why should it even be necessary given that everything bears witness to our being — our friendships and animosities, our glances and handshakes, our memories and all that we forget, our books as well as our pens. For the most important inquiry, however, there is a method. Let the young soul survey its own life with a view to the following question: "What have you truly loved thus far? What has ever uplifted your soul, what has dominated and delighted it at the same time? Assemble these revered objects in a row before you and perhaps they will reveal a law by their nature and their order: the fundamental law of your very self. Compare these objects, see how they complement, enlarge, outdo, transfigure one another; how they form a ladder on whose steps you have been climbing up to yourself so far; for your true self does not lie buried deep within you, but rather rises immeasurably high above {**340/341**} you, or at least above what you commonly take to be your I.

[4b] Your true educators and cultivators[10] will reveal to you the original sense[11] and basic stuff of your being, something

that is not ultimately amenable to education or cultivation by anyone else, but that is always difficult to access, something bound and immobilized; your educators cannot go beyond being your liberators. And that is the secret of all true culture:[12] she does not present us with artificial limbs, wax-noses, bespectacled eyes — for such gifts leave us merely with a sham image[13] of education. She is liberation instead, pulling weeds, removing rubble, chasing away the pests that would gnaw at the tender roots and shoots of the plant; she is an effusion of light and warmth, a tender trickle of nightly rain; sometimes she is imitation and adoration of nature in her motherly and compassionate mood, at other times completion of nature when her cruel and merciless attacks are preempted and turned to good, and when the expressions of her stepmotherly attitude and her doleful irrationality are discretely veiled from view.

[5] There may be other methods for finding oneself, for waking up to oneself out of the anesthesia in which we are commonly enshrouded as if in a gloomy[14] cloud — but I know of none better than that of reflecting upon one's educators and cultivators.[15] And so today I would like to recall the one teacher and master-discipliner[16] in whose memory I glory, *Arthur Schopenhauer* — in order that I might later recall others.

II

[6] As I try to describe what a momentous occasion it was for me to cast my first glance at Schopenhauer's writings, let me dwell a little on an idea that occurred to me, when I was young, more frequently and urgently than any other. When I allowed my wishes to roam to my heart's content back then, I thought to myself that fate might unburden me of the frightful and laborious duty {341/342} of educating myself if only I could, at the right time, find a philosopher who would be my educator, a true philosopher whom I could obey without

hesitation because I could trust him better than myself. Next I asked myself what the principles might be according to which he would educate me, and I pondered what he might say about the two educational maxims that enjoy such a vogue in our times. One demands that an educator quickly identify the particular strengths of his pupils and that he should then direct all their vital powers, all streams of inward energy,[17] and all sunshine towards that end alone, so that a single virtue might be brought to full fruition and fecundity. The second maxim, on the other hand, wants the educator to employ all available powers to nurse them and to bring them into a harmonious relationship with one another. So should someone who has a decided inclination to be a goldsmith therefore be compelled to study music? Should we side with Cellini's[18] father, who kept forcing him to play the flute, which to the father was "that dear little horn" and to the son "that accursed whistle"?[19] Surely it would not be right where talents are so pronounced and clearly expressed — in which case the maxim of harmonious development may be applicable only to weaker natures, in whom a whole host of needs and inclinations may have made their nest, but where none mean much, whether taken individually or as a whole. Yet where do we find such a harmonious wholeness, several voices sounding together in a single nature; where do we admire harmony more than in precisely such men as Cellini, in whom everything — insight, desire, love, hatred — tends towards one center, one powerful root, and in whom a harmonious system of motions, to and fro, up and down, is formed precisely through the coercive, overbearing power that rules from the living center? Might the two maxims turn out, then, not to be in contradiction after all? Perhaps it is only that the one urges man {343/344} to have a center, while the other insists that he must have a periphery, too? That educating philosopher of whom I was dreaming would not only discover the central power, but would also know how to prevent it from acting in a destructive manner on all the other powers. The purpose of his education, it seemed to me, would be to reshape the whole human being into a living, moving solar and planetary system and to identify the law governing its higher mechanics.[20]

[7a] Meanwhile I had to do without my philosopher, and I tried out this and that. I realized how miserable we moderns look beside the Greeks and Romans,[21] even just with respect to how little seriousness and strictness there is in our conception of educational purposes. Yearning for more, one can run from one end of Germany to the other without finding what one is looking for, especially in the universities. Much baser and simpler wishes remain unfulfilled here. One desiring, among Germans, to train himself seriously as a speaker, for example, or someone seeking a school for writers, would not be able to find either masters or schools anywhere.[22] It does not seems to have occurred to anyone here yet that speaking and writing are arts that cannot be acquired without the most careful instruction and the most arduous years of training. The presumptuous complacency of our contemporaries is nowhere more demonstrable and disgraceful than in the sometimes stingy, sometimes thoughtless, but always puny demands they make of educators and teachers. How little suffices, even among our nobler and better-taught types, under the guise of private tutors. What a collection of cranks and outdated methods commonly goes by the name of Gymnasium[23] and meets with our approval. What little we all content ourselves with so far as the highest learning, at the universities, is concerned! What leaders, what institutions, when we set them beside the demanding task of educating a human being to be a human being! Even the widely admired manner in which German scholars go at their research shows first of all that {343/344} they are concerned strictly with science rather than with anything humane, and second that they are trained like a lost flock[24] to sacrifice themselves and to recruit new generations for the same sacrifice. Such a way of dealing with science, unguided and unconstrained by any higher maxims of education, but only let off the leash on the principle

"the more the better," is bound to be as harmful to scholars as is the economic doctrine of laissez-faire to the morality of entire peoples. Who still remembers that the education of a scholar, if his humanity is not to be abandoned and left to die of thirst, is a most delicate problem? The delicacy of which task is made visible to anyone in those many cases where an ill-considered and all-too premature devotion to science has not raised its devotees, but bent them out of shape and honored them with a hump.[25]

[7b] But there is a still more important testimonial for the absence of all higher education, more important and dangerous, and more general. If it is immediately clear why no speaker or writer can now be educated among us (because there are simply no educators for him) and if it is equally evident why a scholar has to turn out crooked and cranky (because it is science, in other words an inhuman abstraction, that is supposed to educate him), then we need to ask at last where any one of us, whether learned or not, noble or not, is supposed to find his ethical examples and celebrities, the visible incarnations of all creative morality in this age and among these contemporaries? What has become of that contemplation of ethical questions which has at all times animated the more nobly developed kinds of human fellowship? There are no such celebrities, there is no such contemplation any more, and we are in fact consuming what we have inherited by way of ethical capital, which was accumulated by our ancestors and which we are no longer able to increase, but only to squander. Such matters are either no longer discussed at all in our {344/345} society, or else it is done with such naturalistic clumsiness and inexperience that it can only arouse disgust. Thus we have arrived at a point where our schools and teachers simply ignore any ethical education, or else resign themselves to mere formalities. Virtue, then, is a word that means nothing to either teachers or students any more, an old-fashioned word that makes one smile — and those who do not smile are even worse, for they must be hypocrites.

[8] The explanation for such feeble-heartedness and the low ebb of all ethical powers is difficult and complicated; but no one who takes into account how a triumphant Christianity has influenced the ethics of our old world will be able to overlook the repercussions of Christianity's defeat, which is becoming ever more probable in our times. Christianity managed, by the loftiness of its ideals, so completely to outdo all ancient moral systems and the universal reign of the natural that men ended up becoming insensitive to and disgusted with the natural. But later, when better and higher things were still recognized but could no longer be attained, there was no way to return to the simple goodness and virtue of the ancients,[26] however much one might have wished it. In this to-and-fro between the Christian and the ancient mode, between a timorous or mendacious Christian morality on the one hand and a dispirited and embarrassed antiquarianism on the other, modern man makes his poor uneasy home. The inherited fear of everything natural, but then also the renewed appeal of the same; the longing for a foothold somewhere, and the impotence of his insights; the endless stumbling from the good to the better and back;[27] all this robs the modern soul of peace and ties it in such knots that it is forever condemned to infertility and joylessness. Never was there a greater need for ethical educators, and never were they harder to find. In times when doctors are most needed, during major epidemics, they are also at the greatest risk. For where are those doctors of {**345/346**} modern mankind who themselves stand so robustly and healthily on their feet that they are able to support others and lead them by the hand? A certain darkening and dulling has befallen even the best personalities of our age, a permanent vexation with the struggle between pretense and sincerity that is being fought out in their breasts, an unrestfulness and lack of confidence in themselves that leaves them altogether unable to show the way to others or to be their master-discipliners.

[9] Thus I was letting my wishes roam very freely, indeed,

if I imagined that I would find a true philosopher for an educator — one who could raise his pupil above the inadequacy of the times and who might once more teach him to be *plain* and *sincere*, in his thinking and his living, that is to say, to be *untimely*, taking that word in its deepest meaning. For human beings have now become so many-sided and complicated that they must be insincere if they want to talk, to assert anything, and to act accordingly.

[10] Such was my plight, such were my needs and desires, when I made the acquaintance of Schopenhauer.[28]

[11a] I am one of those readers of Schopenhauer's who, after reading the first page, knew for sure that they would have to read all others and listen to every word he had ever spoken.[29] I trusted him immediately and I still trust him as much today as I did nine years ago.[30] I understood him as if he had written for me alone, to put it in a way that is easily understood if also immodest and foolish. That is why I have never found anything paradoxical in his work, though here and there a little error; for what are paradoxes other than claims that inspire no confidence, because the author himself made them without much self-assurance, desiring only to appear brilliant, to be seductive, and to make an impression in general? Schopenhauer never concerns himself with how he appears,[31] because he writes for himself, and no one likes to be cheated, least of all a philosopher who has made it his law *to deceive nobody, not even himself!*[32] {346/347} That is, to shun even the agreeable, sociable kind of deception that nearly every conversation entails, which writers in their turn imitate almost without being aware of it, and even more the deliberate deception from the speaker's podium, by the artifices of rhetoric. Far from it: Schopenhauer converses with himself, or if we absolutely must imagine a participant, let us picture a son whom his father wishes to instruct. With forthright, sturdy, good-natured talk he speaks to someone who listens with love. Such writers are missing among us. A powerful sense of well-being envelops us at the first sound of his voice. It is as if we

were entering into a mountain forest: we breathe more deeply and suddenly feel well again. We find that the air is uniformly bracing here; that there is a certain inimitable natural ease, such as men possess who are at home in themselves, as masters over very rich homes, indeed. Contrast those writers who are more surprised than anyone when they manage to come up with something clever, and whose delivery is on that account always anxious and unnatural.

[11b] Nor are we reminded, when we hear Schopenhauer speak, of the scholar who is by nature stiff and narrow-chested and therefore comes across as clumsy, sheepish, or pretentious. On the contrary, Schopenhauer's rugged and somewhat bearish soul[33] teaches us not to miss, indeed to disdain, the smooth and courtly graces of the better French writers. In him one will not find a trace of that imitative, as it were silver-plated pseudo-Gallicism on which German writers pride themselves so. Here and there Schopenhauer reminds me a little of Goethe, but otherwise of nothing German. For he knows how to express profound things simply, moving things without rhetoric, and strictly scientific things without pedantry. From what German could he have learnt as much? He also keeps his distance from the quibbling, floppy, and {347/348} — if I may say so — rather un-German manner of Lessing;[34] which is no small accomplishment considering that Lessing is, in respect of prosaic expression, the most seductive writer among the Germans. Let me start with the very best that could be said of Schopenhauer's way of writing, by referring to his statement that "a philosopher must be very honest if he is to do without any poetical or rhetorical aids." That honesty counts for something, that it might even be a virtue, is one of those private opinions that are prohibited in an age of public opinion. Thus it may not be to praise, but it is certainly to characterize Schopenhauer, when I repeat that he is honest even as a writer, which is true of so few other writers that one ought really to be suspicious of anyone who picks up a pen. I can think of only one other writer whom I

would consider Schopenhauer's equal in sincerity, perhaps even his superior, and that is Montaigne. To think that such a man once wrote is truly to find greater joy in living on this earth. The effect of my acquaintance with the freest and most vigorous of human souls has been such that I can only repeat what he said of Plutarch: "No sooner had I set my eyes upon him than I grew legs or wings."[35] If it were my task to make myself at home on earth, I would choose Montaigne for my companion.

[12] Besides sincerity, Schopenhauer has a second trait in common with Montaigne: a truly cheering cheerfulness.[36] *Aliis laetus, sibi sapiens* [Cheerful unto others, wise unto himself].[37] For there are two very different kinds of cheerfulness. The first, that of a true thinker, always cheers and invigorates us, whether he is speaking in earnest or in jest, whether expressing his human insight or his divine forbearance; without grouchy gestures, trembling hands, or moist eyes, but always firm and simple, with courage and vigor; perhaps with a touch of the knight's hardness,[38] and always as someone victorious. For that is what cheers us most deeply and fervently, to see a god triumphant amidst all the monsters that he has {348/349} overcome.[39] The second kind of cheerfulness, which one may encounter among mediocre writers and short-range thinkers, is only good for leaving one nauseous from reading. Thus my impression of David Strauß, for example.[40] One can only be ashamed of having that kind of cheerful contemporary, who will merely give these times and generations a bad name before posterity. Such cheermongers in fact see nothing of the suffering and the monsters that they pretend to be confronting, and their cheerfulness is distressing because it is fraudulent, because it wishes to mislead us into believing that a victory has been won here.

[12b] For basically there can be cheerfulness only where there is victory, and that goes for the works of all true thinkers as well as for all true works of art. Let the subject matter be as terrible and grave as the problem of existence happens to be, the work will oppress and torment us only when it is a pseudo-

thinker or a pseudo-artist who has doused it with the odor of his inadequacy. Whereas there can be nothing more joyful, nothing better, than to find oneself in proximity to one of those victorious ones who must love what is fullest of life because they have thought what is deepest, and who must turn towards what is beautiful because they are wise. Only they truly speak, without stuttering or empty chattering; only they truly move and truly live, as opposed to the eerie masquerading that otherwise passes for life among human beings. That is why, among such men, we sense something genuinely human and natural for a change, and why we are eager to exclaim with Goethe: "How glorious and delicious is a truly living thing! How well-adapted to its condition, how genuine, how *existing*[41]!"

[13] What I am describing is only the first, as it were physiological, impression that Schopenhauer made on me — that almost magical emission of inner power from one natural creature[42] to another which follows upon the slightest initial contact. And when I analyze that impression with hindsight, I find that it is composed of three elements: {**349/350**} his sincerity, his cheerfulness, and his constancy. He is sincere because he speaks and writes to and for himself; cheerful, because his thinking has overcome the greatest difficulties; constant, because he can be no other way. His strength rises like a flame when there is no wind at all, straight and effortlessly upward, without any wavering, trembling, or restlessness at all. He finds his way no matter what, without anyone noticing him even looking for it, as if some law of gravity were making him run, so firmly and nimbly, so necessarily. Anyone with a sense for what it means, among so many contemporary human tragelaphs,[43] to be a complete, harmonious creature that swings solidly upon its own hinges, full of energy and free of inhibitions, will understand my delight and my amazement when I found Schopenhauer. I could guess that he was the very educator and philosopher for whom I had been searching all those years. I only had his book, of course,[44] and therein lay a

great limitation. So I made a particular effort to see through the book and to imagine the man in flesh whose great testament I had before me, and who would only make heirs of those who wished and were able to be more than mere readers, namely his sons and pupils.

III

[14] THE ESTEEM IN WHICH I HOLD A PHILOSOPHER IS ALWAYS IN proportion to the example he is able to give. That he may by his example draw entire peoples along cannot be doubted: the history of India, which is very nearly the history of Indian philosophy, proves as much.[45] But the example must be visible in a man's life, and not just in his books; his teaching must be done, in other words, in the manner of the ancient Greek philosophers, much more through facial expressions, posture, clothing, diet, and custom than through speaking, let alone writing. Alas, how far we are in Germany from such a courageous visibility of the philosophical life! How very slowly {350/351} our bodies are freeing themselves when our minds seem to have been liberated long ago, though it is mere delusion to imagine that the mind could ever be free and independent so long as the acquired freedom from constraint — which is really the creative freedom to constrain oneself — does not prove itself by every glance and every step, from sunrise to sunset. Kant clung to the university, abased himself before the governments of the day,[46] maintained religious appearances, and tolerated his colleagues and students: so it is only natural that his example has mostly produced university professors and university philosophy.[47] Schopenhauer, by contrast, paid little heed to the learned caste; he distanced himself; he strove for independence from the state and society — that is the example he gives, the ideal he represents, to start at the most superficial level. But there are many degrees in the liberation of philosophical life that remain

unknown among the Germans, and things cannot remain thus forever. Our artists live more boldly and honestly, and the most potent example before us, that of Richard Wagner, shows how a genius must not be afraid to place himself in the most hostile opposition to existing forms and orders if he means to bring the higher order and truth that lives inside him to light among his contemporaries. That "truth" of which there is so much talk among our professors, on the other hand, seems to be a rather undemanding thing that does not frighten anyone with anything disorderly or extraordinary, an easy-going and homely creature eager to reassure the powers that be, again and again, that no one has any inconvenience to fear from what is, after all, only "pure research." Philosophy in Germany will have to start unlearning how to be "pure research": Schopenhauer shows the way.

[15] It is nothing short of a miracle that he could grow into such a human example. For there were tremendous dangers, external as well as internal, crowding in on him, each of which might have crushed or {**351/352**} splintered a weaker creature. I would say that it looked very much as if the man Schopenhauer would perish and leave behind only a remnant, a little "pure research" at most, and likely not even that.

[16a] An Englishman of more recent times discusses the most common danger that faces unusual human beings who must live within societies wedded to all things customary: "Uncongenial minds become first cowed, then melancholy, then out of health, and at last die. A Shelley in New England could hardly have lived, and a race of Shelleys would have been impossible."[48] Our own Hölderlin and Kleist[49] were doomed by their unusualness and could not endure the climate of so-called German culture.[50] Only such iron[51] natures as Beethoven, Goethe, Schopenhauer, and Wagner are able to withstand it, and even their features and wrinkles bear witness to the fatigues of so much struggling and straining;[52] their breathing has lost its natural ease and the tone of their voices gets too sharp all-too easily. An experienced

diplomat, after barely glancing at Goethe and exchanging only a few words, turned to a friend and said: "*Voilà un homme qui a eu de grands chagrins!*" ["There's a man who has had great sorrows!"] Which in Goethe's German[53] reads: "*Das ist auch einer, der sich's hat sauer werden lassen.*" ["There's another one for whom things have gone sour."][54] He adds: "If the vestiges of our past sufferings and actions cannot be erased from our facial features, then it is no wonder if *everything* that remains of us and our purposes will bear the same marks." And that is Goethe talking, the man to whom our cultural philistines[55] like to point as the happiest German of all, thereby proving to their own satisfaction that it is quite possible to live happily among them, with the corollary that no one shall be forgiven for feeling unhappy and lonely in their midst. Thus the maxim, postulated and demonstrated with great cruelty, that there must be secret guilt wherever there is a case of loneliness.

[16b] Poor Schopenhauer, too, bore such {352/353} a secret guilt in his heart, namely that of preferring his philosophy to his contemporaries, and he was unfortunate enough to have learnt from none other than Goethe that if he wished to preserve his philosophy, he would have to defend it at any cost against the disregard of his times. For there is a kind of inquisitorial censorship in which the Germans, according to Goethe, have made great strides: inviolable silence. Among whose signal accomplishments must be counted the fact that most of the first edition of Schopenhauer's great work ended up being pulped.[56] The looming danger that his great deed might simply be undone through neglect left him in a terrible state of agitation that was not easy to tame. Not a single significant follower showed himself. It is saddening to see him hunting for the merest scraps of publicity, and there is something painfully moving about his loud, nay noisy, triumph ("*legor et legar*" [I am read, I shall be read]) when at last he found himself being noticed. It is precisely in those of his features that least suggest the dignity of the philosopher that we can see the suffering human being

who fears for his most precious goods. Thus he was tormented
by the worry that his small fortune might be lost and that he
might have to give up his pure and genuinely ancient attitude
towards philosophy.[57] And thus his longing for truly ingenuous
and compassionate human beings often led him astray, whence
he always returned, with sorrow in his eyes, to his faithful
dog.[58] He was a recluse through and through;[59] not a single
truly likeminded friend consoled him — and there is an infinite
distance between one and none, as always between I-ness and
Nothingness.[60] No one who has real friends can know what
true loneliness is, even if the whole world turned against him.
Alas, I can tell that you have no idea what it means to become
truly lonesome.

[16c] Wherever there have been powerful societies,
governments, religions, public opinions, in short, wherever
there has been tyranny, there the lonely philosopher {353/354}
has been hated. For philosophy offers man a refuge inaccessible
to all tyrants, the den of interior life, the labyrinth of the heart;
and that angers tyrants. Lonely men may hide themselves
there, but it is also where the greatest dangers lie in wait for
them. These men who have escaped inward with their freedom
must still lead an outward life as well, becoming visible and
showing themselves. By birth, domicile, education, fatherland,
chance, and by the importunities of others, they are enmeshed
in countless human connections; countless opinions are
likewise attributed to them simply because they happen to be
the dominant views; every gesture that is not a denial will be
taken for an affirmation; every movement of the hand that does
not smash things up will be understood as a sign of approval.
They know well, these lonely and free spirits, that they will
invariably appear, in one thing or another, to be other than what
they actually are in their thoughts. Desiring nothing but trust
and sincerity, they are caught in a web of misunderstandings.
However great their desire to keep their actions from being
shrouded in a haze of false opinions, accommodations, near-

concessions, kindly omissions, or erroneous interpretations, there is nothing they can do to prevent it.

[16d] Thus a cloud of melancholy gathers on their brows: for such natures hate it more than death itself that we must necessarily *seem*, do what we may; which so embitters them that they become volcanic and menacing. From time to time they take vengeance for the violent self-concealment and self-restraint that has been forced upon them. They emerge from their dens with terrifying grimaces; their words and deeds are explosions then, and it is possible that they will perish of themselves. So dangerously did Schopenhauer live. It is such lonely ones, above all, who need love, who need companions before whom they may be as open and plain as they are before themselves, and in whose presence the tensions of restrained silence and pretense are dissolved. Take away these companions and there will be a growing danger. Heinrich von Kleist, for example, was doomed because he was unloved,[61] and the most terrible {354/355} means to use against unusual men is to drive them so deeply into themselves that every reemergence of theirs must turn into an eruption. Every now and then a demigod arises who can endure life even under such terrible conditions, and who can even live triumphantly.[62] To hear his lonely song, listen to Beethoven's music.[63]

[17a] So much for the first danger in whose shadow Schopenhauer grew up: that of becoming lonesome. The second was that he might despair of the truth, a danger that must beset any thinker who takes the Kantian philosophy as his starting point, provided that he is vigorous and complete human being, full of suffering and longing, and not just a clattering calculator or thought-machine.[64] Alas, we all know only too well how much cause for shame there is in this latter precondition: for it seems to me that there are only a very few cases in which Kant's thought has actually come alive and been transformed into blood and other vital juices. It is everywhere alleged, of course, that the deeds of this quiet scholar are supposed to

have started a revolution in all domains of knowledge; but I do not believe it. For when I look at the men around me, I see no clear indication that anyone's self has been revolutionized, which would need to be the first step before entire regions could undergo a revolution. If Kant ever actually began to have a popular impact, it would become visible to us in the form of a nagging, corrosive skepticism and relativism; which would be replaced, only among the most active and noble spirits, who have never been able to endure doubt for long, by the kind of upheaval and despair of all truth that Kleist, for one, experienced as a consequence of his exposure to the Kantian philosophy: "A little while ago," he once wrote in his moving manner, "I became acquainted with the Kantian philosophy — and now I must share a thought about it without getting afraid that it will prove as profoundly painful and devastating to you as it was for me. It is this: we cannot resolve whether what we call truth really is {**355/356**} truth, or whether it only seems such to us. If the latter, then the truth that we gather here will be nothing after death, and all striving for possessions that might follow us to the grave is in vain. If the sharp point of this thought does not pierce your heart, do not smile at one who has been wounded deep down in his most sacred inward parts. My only, my highest goal has sunk and I have no other."[65] When will human beings be able to feel in such a natural Kleistian manner again, when will they relearn to measure the meaning of a philosophy by their "most sacred inward parts"? This we need to know before we can begin to gauge just what Schopenhauer, coming after Kant, can be for us — namely the guide who will lead us, after having been the first to lead himself there, from the caverns of skeptical discontent and the self-denial of criticism up towards the heights of tragic contemplation, the starry night-sky endless above us.[66]

[17b] Therein lies the greatness of Schopenhauer, in that he confronted the picture of life as a whole in order to interpret it in its entirety, while our cleverest minds cannot be dissuaded

from the folly of thinking that one can arrive at a better interpretation by a painstaking examination of the colors, the paint, and the canvas — perhaps concluding that the fabric is of a most intricate weave and the paint of a chemical composition that is beyond the reach of science. Schopenhauer, by contrast, knew that one must make the right guesses about the painter if one is to understand the painting. Meanwhile the whole guild of scientists aims at understanding the canvas and the paint, but not the picture. Hence it might even be said that only someone who keeps his eyes firmly fixed on the great painting of life and existence can make use of the individual sciences without harming himself, because without such a regulative image of the whole, the sciences become mere ropes[67] that never lead to any end and that serve only to confuse the course of our life and make it a labyrinth. Herein, once again, lies Schopenhauer's greatness, in that he pursues the whole picture as Hamlet does the {356/357} ghost, without letting himself be fobbed off, as scholars do, or getting distracted by any scholasticism of terminology, which is the fate of all untamed dialecticians. The study of all quarter-philosophies[68] is appealing only insofar as it allows us to see how they immediately pounce upon those sections in the edifice of a great system of thought where one may indulge oneself in scholarly pros and cons, where it is permissible to mull, to doubt, to argue, and where the demand of all great philosophy is evaded, which in its entirety always says only one thing: "This is the picture of all life, and from it you must learn the meaning of your existence. And conversely: read only from your own life, and thereby understand the hieroglyphs of life in general."

[17c] And thus Schopenhauer's philosophy, too, should be understood: by the individual for himself, in order to gain insight into his own misery and needfulness, his own limitedness, and then to get acquainted with the antidotes and consolations, such as making a sacrifice of one's ego and submitting to the noblest motivations, among which justice and mercy take pride

of place. Schopenhauer teaches us to distinguish between the real and the merely apparent causes of human happiness: how neither riches nor honors nor scholarly learning can raise one above desponding over the worthlessness of one's existence, and how the striving for such worldly goods can become meaningful only when it is illumined by a higher, more complete purpose, namely that of attaining self-mastery in order to help one's physical being along and to correct its follies and blunders a little. All this only for oneself, in the beginning; but eventually, through oneself, for everyone. Admittedly such an ambition may lead to a deep and heartfelt resignation: for what and how much can we really hope to improve at all, either individually or more generally?

[18] If we apply these words to Schopenhauer, we touch upon the third and most characteristic danger in which he lived and which lay hidden in his very build and bones. Every human being is wont to discover such limitations within himself, whether in what his meager talents leave him unable to do or in what his moral shortcomings leave him unable to want,[69] {357/358} as must fill him with yearning and melancholy; and just as a sense of his own sinfulness will leave a man yearning for all that is holy, so he bears within himself, as an intellectual being, a deep craving for genius. Here lies the root of all true culture: in man's yearning to be *reborn* as a saint or genius, which one can easily understand, in mythical terms, without first becoming a Buddhist.[70] Where we encounter ability without such yearning, in scholarly circles or among so-called learned men, we are repelled and disgusted, because we can sense that such men, for all their brains, do not help culture to develop, but rather hinder it and prevent the arising of genius that is its very goal. What we have here is a case of petrification that is as unworthy as that merely habitual, frigid, and conceited virtuousness which is the furthest from true holiness and keeps it at bay. Now Schopenhauer's nature was split in a most peculiar and dangerous way. Few thinkers have felt to such a degree and

with such incomparable assurance as he that genius was alive within them; and his genius made him the highest promise: that there would be no deeper furrow than the one he was plowing into the soil of modern mankind. So one half of his being was thoroughly sated and fulfilled, equally free of desire and sure of its power, and he answered with greatness and dignity to the calling of one perfected in victory.[71] Only in the other half there remained a tempestuous yearning, which we might discern when we hear that he averted his pained gaze from a picture of the great founder of the Trappist order, Jean de Rancé, with the words: "That is a matter of grace."[72] For a genius yearns more deeply for holiness because from his perch he has seen further and more clearly than other men: down into the reconciliation of insight and being; across the kingdom of peace and of the negated will; and over the waters towards that other bank of the river of which the Indians speak.[73] Here we have a miracle: for how incredibly whole and {358/359} unbreakable must Schopenhauer's nature have been if it could not be destroyed by such a yearning and did not become hardened either. What that means we may all understand according to what and how much we amount to, though none of us will understand it completely, in its full gravity.

[19] The more one ponders the three dangers I have outlined above, the more astonished one must be at how robustly Schopenhauer was able to defend himself against them and at how healthy and straight he remained when he emerged from the fight. With many scars and open wounds, granted, and in a mood that was perhaps a little rough, and at times rather too war-like. Above even the greatest human being, there looms his own ideal. But that Schopenhauer can be a model for us, that much is certain, all scars and blemishes notwithstanding. One is even tempted to say that the flawed and all-too human aspects of his being are just what will allow us to draw near to him in the most human sense, for thus we are able to see him as someone who suffered, as a companion in our miseries, and

not just as someone set apart from us by the forbidding majesty of his genius.

[20] Three dangers that threatened Schopenhauer's constitution threaten us all. Each of us bears within himself, at the core of his being, some productive uniqueness that will give him a bright and unfamiliar aura, that of the unusual, as soon as he becomes aware of what is so unique about himself. Which is something that the majority of men will find intolerable because they are lazy, as I have said, and because every uniqueness brings with it a chain of troubles and burdens. There is no doubt that the unusual man who takes that chain upon himself will thereby forsake most of what he expected of life in his youth: cheerfulness, security, ease, honor. He will become lonesome: that is how his fellow human beings will reward him; the desert and the cave will beckon no matter where he may choose to live. Now he must guard himself against the first danger, that of getting subdued, against becoming downcast and melancholy. Therefore he may want to surround himself with images of those good and brave fighters of which Schopenhauer was one. Then {359/360} there was a second danger, also by no means rare, that confronted Schopenhauer. Here and there we find a man whom nature has armed with a sharp mind that inclines him to the double-dealing of dialectics. How easy it is for him, if he is incautious enough to give free rein to his abilities, to be destroyed as a human being and become a ghost whose life is confined to "pure research." Or else he may, owing to his habit of seeking out every pro and con in things, be driven mad by his quest for truth and end up living without courage or confidence, negating, doubting, nagging, malcontented, half-hoping, half-expecting to be disappointed: "No dog could bear to live like this!"[74] The third danger is the ethical or intellectual petrification that results when a man tears asunder the bond that unites him with his ideal, when he ceases to be fruitful and to multiply in his domain, and when he thus becomes weak and useless for the purposes of culture. The uniqueness of his being

has become an indivisible, incommunicable atom: where once there was lava,[75] now there is cold rock. And so a man may be ruined by his uniqueness as well as by his fear of the same, by holding on to himself as well as by giving himself up, by his own yearning as well as by his own petrification. For to be alive is to be endangered.

[21a] Besides the dangers inherent in Schopenhauer's whole constitution, to which he would have been exposed whatever century he might have lived in, there were also the dangers that arose for him out of his *times*; and it is important to bear in mind this distinction between constitutional and temporal dangers if we want to comprehend what is so exemplary and educational about Schopenhauer's nature. Let us imagine the eye of the philosopher resting upon existence: he means to reappraise its value and fix it at a new rate. For it has always been the peculiar task of great thinkers to be the legislators for measures and weights and the standards of coinage that apply to all things.[76] What a hindrance it must be to him, then, if mankind, as it is revealed to him in his immediate surroundings, should turn out to be a puny fruit riddled with wormholes! How much he must include, if he wants to do justice to existence in general, {360/361} in tallying up the full sum of his own age's unworthiness! If it is worthwhile to study the history of past or foreign peoples, then it is so most of all for the philosopher who wishes to pass judgment on the lot of mankind as a whole, and who would be just not only towards the average, but more especially towards the *highest* lot that can befall either single men or entire peoples. Because the present will always force itself upon us, because it attracts and commands the eye, whether the philosopher likes it or not, it will invariably be estimated at too high a value in the final reckoning. That is why the philosopher must be especially careful when assessing his own age in contrast with others: it is only after he has been able to overcome the present within himself that he that he can also overcome the present in his picture of life, namely by making it

unremarkable, and indeed by painting it over.

[21b] It is a great, almost an insurmountable challenge. The judgment of the ancient Greek philosophers about the value of existence counts for so much more than any modern judgment because they had life itself before them and around them in such abundant perfection, and because with them a thinker's feelings did not, as they do with us, get tied in knots over the tension[77] between the wish for freedom, beauty, greatness of life, on the one hand, and the urge[78] towards truth, which asks only what existence is ultimately worth,[79] on the other. It remains important for all ages to know what Empedocles had to say about existence[80] amidst the most vigorous and exuberant joy of life, that of Greek culture; his judgment carries the greatest weight, especially considering that none of the other great philosophers of the same great age ever contradicted him. Empedocles speaks most clearly, but at bottom — if only one opens one's ears a little — they all say the same thing. A modern thinker, on the other hand, will always suffer from an unfulfillable wish: he will ask to be reminded of life — true, red, healthy life such as it existed in the past — before handing down his sentence. For his own part, at least, he will find it necessary to be a living human being {361/362} before he can trust himself to be a just judge. That is why some of the most potent promoters of life, of the will to life today, are modern philosophers, and why they have such a yearning to be raised out of their exhausted age into a real culture that will once more exalt physical being.[81] But this yearning is also their *danger*: in it the reformer of life clashes with the philosopher, that is to say, with the judge of life. However the battle may turn out, the victory will be one that entails a loss as well. How was it that Schopenhauer escaped even that danger?

[22a] So long as every great man would like to be seen as the truest child of his age,[82] and so long as he will suffer more strongly and acutely from its afflictions than his inferiors, so long must the struggle of such a man appear as no more than

a senseless and destructive fight against himself. But those are only appearances, because what he is fighting in his age is just what is keeping him from being great, which in his case means that he fights only to be free and to be entirely himself. Thus his enmity is at bottom directed against that which may be inside him, but which is not essentially part of himself; against the impure confusion and the false association of elements that are incongruous and for ever incompatible; against something time-bound that has been fraudulently soldered to that which is *untimely* about him. And so the supposed child of time[83] turns out, in the end, to be merely its *step-child*. Thus Schopenhauer's striving, from the earliest days of youth, was directed against that false, vain, and unworthy mother, Time,[84] and by casting her out of himself, he cleansed and healed the core of his being[85] and thereby rediscovered himself in his own health and purity. The writings of Schopenhauer must be used as a mirror of time: surely it is not the fault of the mirror if all that is time-bound is reflected in the form of a disfiguring malady, all pallor and emaciation, with hollow eyes and sunken features, the visible marks of a stepchild's sufferings.

[22b] The yearning for vigorous nature, for wholesome and plain {362/363} humanity, was in Schopenhauer a yearning for himself, and as soon as he had defeated time in himself, he was bound to discover, with an amazed glance, the genius dwelling there. The secret at the core of his being had been revealed; his stepmother Time had been foiled in her efforts to hide his own genius from him; the kingdom of exalted physical life[86] had been discovered. When he now turned his fearless gaze towards the question of what existence is ultimately worth,[87] he no longer needed to concern himself with evaluating a confused and pallid time and judging its hypocritical and murky way of life. He knew full well that there are higher and purer things to be found and attained on this earth than such a time-bound[88] life, and that it would be a bitter injustice to know and judge life only by such an ugly manifestation. No, let us now call upon

the genius himself so that we might hear whether he is able to justify the highest fruits of life, and perhaps life in general. The glorious[89] creative man shall answer this question: "Do you affirm this existence from the bottom of your heart? Does it suffice for you? Will you be its champion, its redeemer? Only say the word and a single truthful 'Yes!' from your mouth shall free that Life which stands so gravely accused." What will he answer? The answer of Empedocles.[90]

IV

[23] NEVER MIND IF THE LAST HINT REMAINS A LITTLE OPAQUE; right now I am getting at something very easily understood, namely how we may all use Schopenhauer to educate ourselves *against our times* — because we have the advantage, through him, of really *knowing* our times. If it is indeed an advantage! At any rate, it may no longer be possible a few centuries from now. I take delight in imagining that human beings will soon tire of their books and writers and that one day a scholar will come to his senses, make his will, and provide for his corpse to be {**363/364**} burned on a pyre made of his tomes, his own writings topmost. What with our forests getting ever scarcer, will it not be time, before long, to use our libraries for firewood, for straw and kindling? Since most books are made of smoke and steam anyway, why not return them to same condition? Let them be punished by fire for not containing any fire within them. And so it is quite possible that the future may look back upon our age as a Dark Age [*saeculum obscurum*[91]] because its products so enticed us to throw them into the oven. How lucky we may therefore count ourselves that we still have a chance to get to know this age. For if it ever makes sense to concern oneself with one's age, then it must be a blessing to do so as thoroughly as possible, lest anything remain doubtful about it. And that is what Schopenhauer allows us to do.

[24] Granted, we would be a hundred times luckier still if our examination were to reveal that no age ever gave greater cause for pride and hope than our own. And there are some naive folks in remote parts of the earth, say in Germany, who are ready to believe just such a thing, who say quite seriously that the world was set right a couple of years ago[92] and that anyone who might harbor grave doubts about existence has been proved wrong by the "facts." There it is: with the foundation of the new German Reich, we are told, the decisive, devastating blow has been struck against all "pessimistic" philosophizing, and that is supposed to be that. So if anyone wishes to answer the question what it might mean for a philosopher to be an educator in our times, he must first respond to that view, which is very widespread and much-cherished, especially in the universities. Let it be done like this: *It is a disgrace and an outrage that such a disgusting, idolatrous flattery of our times could possibly be voiced and repeated by so-called thinking and respectable human beings!* {364/365} What it proves is that men today do not have so much as an inkling of how far the serious business of philosophy is removed from the serious business of the newspapers. Such human beings have forfeited not only the last remnants of philosophy, but the remains of religion as well, and what they have bargained for instead is not optimism, as they imagine, but journalism — the spirit of the day and the dailies, or rather, the lack thereof. Any philosophy that would have us believe that a political event can shift or even solve the problem of existence must be a jest, or else it is an excrescence.[93] The founding of a state is nothing very new in the world; that drama has been staged many times before. How could a political renewal suffice for making men merry dwellers on this earth once and for all? If anyone can really believe such a thing to be possible, let him identify himself: he truly deserves to be made a professor of philosophy at a German university, like Harms in Berlin, Jürgen Meyer in Bonn, and Carrière in Munich.[94]

[25] What we see here are the consequences of the doctrine,

lately preached from every rooftop, that the state is the highest end of mankind and that there can be no higher duty for a man than to serve the state. Which I take to be a relapse not into paganism, but into idiocy. It is possible that a man who sees his services to the state as his highest duty would indeed be unaware of any higher obligations; but there are nonetheless men and duties that go further — and one such duty, which I at least take to be higher than any duty towards the state, is the call to demolish stupidity in all its forms, including this one. That is why I am dealing here with a kind of man whose teleology points a little further than the welfare of the state, namely with the philosopher, and with a world that is largely independent of the state, namely the world of culture. Of the many rings that make for a human community when they are linked up to each other, some are made of gold, others of tombac.[95] {**365/366**}

[26] How, then, would a philosopher look upon the culture of our age? Very differently, to be sure, from those merry professors of philosophy who are so comfortable in their states. To the philosopher it would look as if our culture were in the process of being uprooted and nearly driven to extinction by our universal breathlessness, the ever-increasing velocity of life, and the loss of all leisurely contemplation[96] and simplicity. The waters of religion are ebbing away, leaving behind swamps or puddles. The nations are once again riven with enmity and desire only to tear one another apart. The sciences are rushing ahead without measure and in the spirit of the blindest laissez-faire, shattering and dissolving all that was believed to be solid.[97] Meanwhile the well-schooled classes and states are allowing themselves to be swept along by the splendors of contempt and commerce.[98] Never was the world more worldly, and never was it poorer in love and kindness. No longer do the learned serve as beacons or refuges amidst the ever-worldlier unrest; they, too, are becoming more restless, more thoughtless, more loveless by the day. Everything tends towards the barbarism of the future, today's arts and sciences included. The well-schooled man has

degenerated into the greatest enemy of education, because he persists in denying the illness before the doctors and getting in their way. They get bitterly vexed, these pitiful strutting scoundrels, when one exposes their weakness or resists their pernicious mendacity. They would have us believe that they have won first prize in the great race of the centuries, and there is an artificial jolliness to all their movements. Their way of faking happiness can be a little touching because their happiness is so very incomprehensible. One even hesitates to confront them with the question Tannhäuser asks Biterolf, "What delights have you poor wretch ever enjoyed?"[99] For we know better, alas. The frost of winter is upon our day, and we live beside the cragged mountains where danger is rife and provisions are scarce. Our joys are fleeting and all sunlight pales as it creeps down to us from the white peaks above. Suddenly there is music, an old man cranks his barrel-organ and dancers twirl about — a shocking thing for the lone wanderer[100] to witness: everything that surrounds him is so wild, so inaccessible, {**366/367**} so colorless, so hopeless; yet now the air is ringing with the sound of joy, of thoughtless, noisy joy! Alas, the mists of early evening are already lurking; soon the music falls silent and only the wanderer's steps grind on.[101] As far as the eye can see, nothing remains but the barren and harsh face of nature.

[27a] If it be thought too one-sided for us to focus only on the feebleness of the lines and the dullness of the colors in the picture of modern life, we may turn to the other side, but only to discover that it is by no means more pleasing, but rather more alarming still. Certainly there are great forces at play, enormous forces — wild, primaeval, entirely merciless — upon which one can only look with expectant trepidation, as upon the cauldron in a witches' kitchen. Any moment there might be a flash, a bolt of lightning that announces the advent of new terrors. The past hundred years have been preparing us for all manner of fundamental upheavals, and recent efforts at setting up the powers of the so-called nation-state as a bulwark

against the modern tendency towards collapse or explosion will only aggravate the general insecurity and foreboding for the foreseeable future. The fact that so many individuals carry on as if they knew nothing of such worries need not detain us: their agitation reveals clearly enough what they really think. Thus we see them more frenzied and more obsessed with their own little affairs than human beings have ever been. They build and plant only for the day, and the pursuit of happiness will never be more urgent than when the quarry must be hunted down before nightfall since the day after the hunting season may be over for good. Thus we live in the age of the atom, of atomized chaos.

[27b] During the Middle Ages, warring forces were generally held together and more or less assimilated to one another by the great pressure brought to bear upon them by the Church. When that bond was broken, the forces rose up against one another with all the old fury. The Reformation declared many things to be *adiaphora*, that is *indifferent*, in the sense of not falling under the immediate jurisdiction of religious principles. That was {367/368} the price at which Protestantism bought its right to exist, just as Christianity had once purchased its survival, at a similar price, from a much more religious age.[102] The chasm between the worldly and the religious realms has kept widening, and today nearly everything on earth is determined by the most brutal and vile forces only, namely by the egotism of property-owners and the despotism of the military. In the hands of the military despots, the state seeks to reorganize everything in its own image[103] — as does the egotism of the property-owners[104] — and thus to be the new bond by which pressure is kept on the warring forces. In other words, the state wants men to serve it with the same idolatrous devotion with which they once worshiped the Church. With what success remains to be seen. As yet we are still floating among the ice-shoals in the great stream of the Middle Ages. The thaw has set in and everything has been set in massive, devastating motion, one towering block of ice crashing into another, the banks flooded and endangered.

Revolution is inescapable: the atomic revolution. Which will turn out to be the smallest indivisible particles of modern society?

[28] There is no doubt that when such periods are approaching, *that which is humane*[105] is perhaps in even greater danger than during the actual collapse and the chaotic turbulences themselves. Fearful anticipation and the greedy exploitation of every remaining minute is bound to bring out every craven and selfish impulse of the soul, while real calamities, especially when they are truly great and shared in common, tend rather to improve men and leave them more empathetic. In light of these dangers facing our times, who will serve as the guardians and paladins of *the Humane*,[106] that inviolably sacred treasure gradually accumulated in the common temple of mankind by the successive generations of man? Who will uphold the *image of man* when all around his contemporaries are degenerating to the point of beastliness — succumbing to wormlike selfishness and doglike fear — and even lower to the dead rigidity of mere machines?

[29] There are three images of man that our modern age has posited one after the other so that mortal men may for a long time yet have occasion for exalting their own lives by contemplating them: there is Rousseau's man, Goethe's man, and lastly Schopenhauer's man. The first image has most fire in it and is sure to have the most popular impact. The second is intended only for the few, namely for those who are contemplative natures in the grand style; the masses will only misunderstand it. The third requires the most active men as its viewers: only they may gaze upon it without harm; the easy-going will find it enervating, the masses repellent. Behind the first of our images there is the force that drives mankind towards tempestuous revolutions, past and present; for underneath all the socialist quaking and shaking of the earth, it has always been Rousseau's man agitating things like old Typhos beneath the Aetna.[107] Oppressed and half-crushed by haughty lords and

merciless wealth, made coarse and contemptible in their own eyes by priests, bad upbringings, and ridiculous customs, men in their despair call upon "sacred Nature" and suddenly feel that she is as remote from them as any Epicurean god.[108] Their prayers do not reach her, so deeply has mankind sunk into the chaos of the unnatural. With a sneer, man then casts off all the glittering finery that he considered his most human possession not long before: his arts and sciences, the advantages of a refined life. He beats his fists against the walls in whose shadows he has degenerated and cries for light — for sun, forest, soaring rock. And when he calls out, "Only nature is good, only natural man is human," he despises himself and yearns to go beyond himself; a mood in which the soul is ready for the most terrible decisions, but in which it may also bring to the surface what is noblest and rarest in its depths.

[30a] Goethe's man is no such menacing force; indeed he may, in a certain sense, be called a quieting corrective {369/370} for that dangerous excitement to which Rousseau's man is so prone. When Goethe was young, he clung to the Gospel of Good Nature with all his love-rich heart; his *Faust* was the highest and most daring depiction of Rousseau's man, at least insofar as there was any way of conveying his ravenous hunger for life, his dissatisfaction and yearning, his dealings with the demons of the heart. Let us look what resulted from all this gathering of clouds — certainly no bolt of lightning! What is revealed to us here is precisely a new image of man, that of Goetheian man. One might have thought that Faust should be presented as the champion of hard-pressed life, as an insatiable rebel and liberator, as the personification of the power that negates out of goodness, as the quintessential genius of subversion, equally religious and demonic, in contrast to his quite undemonic companion,[109] of whom he cannot rid himself and whose skeptical wickedness and negativity he must despise even as he uses them for his own ends — the tragic lot of all rebels and liberators. But one would have been mistaken to expect

any such thing. Goethe's man carefully avoids the company of Rousseau's man because he hates violence and all great leaps — and thus all great deeds. Thus the liberator of the world, Faust, becomes a mere world-traveler. The insatiable voyeur flies past all the dominions of life and nature, past all histories, arts, myths, and past all sciences; his deepest desires are excited and placated, even Helen can hold him no longer[110] — and now the moment must come for which his scornful companion has been waiting. At some point the flight must end, the wings must fall,[111] and Mephistopheles is ready. When a German ceases to be Faust, there is no greater danger than that he may turn philistine and go to the devil — only the powers of heaven can save him.

[30b] Goethe's man is, as I have said, contemplative man in the grand style, who can keep himself from wasting away on earth only by {370/371} gathering together for his nourishment all that has ever been great and remarkable and by living as if there were nothing to life but one desire after another. He is not a man of action; whenever he takes his place among active men in the prevailing order of things, one can be sure that nothing worthwhile will come of it — witness Goethe's own zeal for the theater — and that nothing "orderly" will be upset. Goethe's man is a conserving and conciliating force, as much at risk of degenerating into a philistine as Rousseau's man is of turning into a Catilinarian.[112] Only add a little more muscle and natural wildness, and all the virtues of the former would be enhanced. It seems that Goethe knew well wherein the dangers and shortcomings of his kind of man lay, as he hints in Jarno's words to Wilhelm Meister: "It is all very well that you are so morose and bitter; if only you were to become properly vicious for a change, it would be better still."[113]

[31a] To put it bluntly: it is necessary that we all become properly vicious for a change, so that things might get better. The image of Schopenhauerian man should be an encouragement to us in doing so. Such a man takes the voluntary suffering of

truthfulness upon himself, and what he suffers helps him to subdue his egocentrism and to prepare the complete revolution and reversal in his nature that is the essential meaning of life. His unguarded expression of what is true may sound inexcusable to other men, because they consider the preservation of their half-truths and inanities to be a matter of humane duty. One would have to be evil, they think, to want to destroy their toys. To anyone of that sort, they would be tempted to cry out what Faust said to Mephistopheles: "How dare you frigid fiend raise your fist against the teeming, healing powers of Creation?"[114] Anyone aspiring to live according to the Schopenhauerian ideal would probably look more like a Mephistopheles than a Faust {371/372} — at least to myopic modern eyes that cannot see more than evil in a negation.

[31b] But there is a way of negating and destroying that springs precisely from a powerful yearning for sanctification and redemption, and Schopenhauer was the first philosophical teacher to appear with that message before us profane and utterly secularized modern human beings. All existence that can be negated also deserves to be negated.[115] To live most truly would be to believe in an existence that cannot be negated at all because it is so true and free of all falsehood. That is why the man who is truthful in the highest sense finds a metaphysical meaning in his actions, a meaning that can be explained by laws of a superior kind and that is affirming in the most profound sense even if it appears to break and destroy the laws of this life. The actions of such a man must involve him in continuous suffering, but he knows what Meister Eckhart did: "The beast that will carry you most swiftly towards perfection is suffering."[116] I would think that anyone who places such a direction of life before his soul would feel his heart opening up with the fervent desire to be a Schopenhauerian man; that is, to be marvelously pure and serene and altogether unworried about his own welfare; to be consumed with the fire of insight burning within him; to be far removed from the cold and contemptuous neutrality of the so-

called scientific man; to be raised high above any grouchy and morose outlook; to be always prepared for offering himself up as the first sacrifice to the revealed truth; and to be permeated to his core with the awareness of how much suffering must result from such truthfulness.

[31c] Certainly, such a man will destroy his worldly prospects by his courage; he will have to be hostile even towards the human beings he loves best and the institutions that nurtured him; he must not spare either men or things, even if it hurts him to be injuring them; and he will be misunderstood and long mistaken for an accomplice of powers that he in fact abominates. {372/373} When he is judged by common human standards, he will be found unjust even while he is striving for nothing but justice; but he may reassure and console himself with the words of Schopenhauer, his great educator: "A happy life is impossible:[117] the most a man can achieve in this world is to *chart a heroic course through life*.[118] To live thus is to fight on behalf of all, whatever one's particular manner or cause, and to do so against overwhelming opposition and for little or no reward when one emerges victorious at last. In the end such a man will be left standing like the prince in Carlo Gozzi's 'The Stag-King,' petrified, but retaining his noble posture and magnanimous bearing.[119] His memory remains to be celebrated by later generations as that of a hero; his will, mortified by a lifetime of troubles and labors, by paltry success and the ingratitude of the world, is extinguished in Nirvana."[120]

[31d] Of course such a heroic life and the mortification wrought upon it hardly corresponds to the feeble ideas of those who give the longest speeches at festivities commemorating great men and who believe that great men must be great in just the same way as they themselves are small. As if greatness were just given as a present, for a man's own entertainment, or as if it were attained mechanically by a blind obedience to some inner compulsion; so that he who does not receive any present and feels no compulsion might claim the same right to

be small that another has to be great. "Given as a present" or "by compulsion": these are disdainful words spoken so that by slighting those who have heard the call to greatness one might evade any such call oneself. In fact great men are least amenable to presents or compulsion; they know as well as others how one can make an easy life for oneself, how soft a bed awaits anyone who is prepared to get along with his neighbors in the polite and ordinary fashion. For all human order is designed to prevent life from being *felt*, by continuously distracting our minds. {373/374} Why does the great man have such a strong desire for the opposite, namely for feeling life, that is to say, for suffering from life? Because he realizes that he is at risk of being cheated out of himself, that there is a kind of conspiracy to lure him from his own cave.[121] So he balks, pricks up his ears, and decides: "I will hold on to myself!" It is a terrible resolution, as he soon realizes. For now he must plunge down into the very depths of existence[122] with a number of unusual questions on his lips: "Why am I alive? What lessons am I supposed to learn from life? How have I become what I am, and why does what I am cause me so much suffering?"

[31e] So he torments himself as nobody else seems to be doing. Meanwhile he watches his contemporaries passionately convulsing themselves before every phantom scene staged for them in the theater of politics, or he sees them strutting about in a hundred masks,[123] parading as young men or grown men or old men, as fathers, citizens, priests, civil servants, or businessmen, ever so intent on their collective comedy while showing not the least interest in themselves. Asked why it is that they are alive, they would all answer quickly and with pride: "So that I may *become* a good citizen, a scholar, or a statesman." And yet *what they are now* will never be anything other *than it is*, so why be *that* poor thing and not something better? A man who understands his life as no more than a point in the evolution of a family or a state or a science, who therefore wishes to be entirely swallowed up by the story of becoming, by history, has failed to understand

the lesson that existence has assigned him, and he will have to repeat it.[124] The eternal spectacle of becoming is nothing but a treacherous puppet-show that makes men forget themselves; a real distraction[125] that draws the individual out of himself and scatters him in all directions; an endless game of trifles put on for us, and put over on us, by that oversized infant Time. To be heroically truthful, then, is nothing other than to stop being a plaything.

[31f] Everything about *becoming* is hollow, deceptive, shallow, and deserving of our contempt; the riddle that man is meant to solve can be solved only from within *being*, {374/375} by being just what one is and nothing else, in timeless abiding.[126] Now a man may begin to examine how deeply he is connected with becoming, and how deeply with being, and thus an enormous challenge arises before his soul: to destroy all that is mere becoming, to drag everything that is false about things into the light. He, too, wishes for complete insight, but in a different way than the Goetheian man, not for the sake of a noble delicateness, so that he might preserve himself and delight in the delicious diversity of things, but rather by being his own first sacrifice. The heroic man looks with disdain upon whether he is well or unwell, upon his own virtues and vices, upon the whole business of reducing the world to the puny measure of man. He hopes for nothing from himself and wishes to look upon that very bottom of things where hope has no place. His strength lies in his ability to forget himself, and when he does remember himself, he scans the distance between himself and his lofty goal and sees only soot and dregs behind and below himself.

[31g] The ancient thinkers sought with all their might to discover happiness and truth — and no one shall ever find what he has to search for, says the harsh decree of nature.[127] Instead, let a man search out untruth everywhere, let him be willing to welcome unhappiness freely, and perhaps he will find himself miraculously dis-illusioned[128] in a different sense: something

inexpressible may come within his reach, something beside which our concepts of happiness and truth are mere idolatrous images; the world sheds its heaviness, the affairs and powers that be on earth fade like dreams, and everything around him is bathed in the gentle radiance of a summer's eve. To the observer it looks as if he is just beginning to wake and as if what he is seeing at play around him are merely the thinning clouds of a dissolving dream. These, too, will soon have wafted away, and then it will be day.[129]

[32a] I promised that I would go by my own experiences and depict Schopenhauer as an *educator*, so far as the imperfect strokes of my brush will permit. Therefore it cannot be enough for me to paint merely {**375/376**} the human ideal that enveloped him — his Platonic idea, as it were. I will have to do something much more difficult and show how one might gain a *new circle of duties* if one were guided by that ideal; how one might draw close to so ambitious an end through regular activity; in short how one might be *educated* by the ideal. For otherwise it might appear to be no more than a gladdening or even intoxicating view that grants us a few moments of bliss only in order to let us down soon after and leave us feeling all the more despondent. It is true that our *initial* dealings with the Schopenhauerian ideal must follow a pattern that is as old as our ideals themselves — light alternating with darkness, our ecstasy with our disgust — but that is merely the threshold over which we should not linger; let us step quickly through the doorway and beyond our first beginnings.

V

[32b] THUS WE NEED TO ASK OURSELVES SERIOUSLY AND RESOLUTELY whether it is possible for such an incredibly lofty end to be brought close enough that it might educate us as it pulls us upward, lest Goethe's great pronouncement be fulfilled: "Man

is born to limitation. He can understand simple, immediate, definite ends and he is accustomed to using those means that are close at hand; but only place things at a distance, and he no longer knows either what he wants or what he ought to do. Nor does it matter whether it is the wealth of options distracting him or whether the loftiness and dignity of certain ends is putting him out of sorts.[130] He is doomed to misfortune whenever he is driven to strive for something to which he cannot draw close by his own regular activity."[131] Thus it may seem a very legitimate objection against Schopenhauerian man that his very dignity and loftiness can only put us out of sorts and place us outside any community of active men; that it makes our duties lose their coherence and leaves the flow of life blocked-up. One man might take his sullen leave {376/377} and get used to living by a double standard and in contradiction to himself, insecure wherever he turns and therefore more enfeebled and infertile by the day. Another man may decide to refrain from action as a matter of principle and get to the point where he can barely endure seeing others act at all. Great dangers arise whenever things are made too difficult for human beings and when they are no longer able to *fulfill* their duties. Thus the stronger natures may perish, while the weaker and more numerous ones sink into easy-going lethargy and finally lose even their ease to their laziness.

[33] In addressing that objection, let me grant that our work has barely begun. Judging by my own experience, there is only one thing I see and know for certain: that it is quite possible for us to submit to a chain of fulfillable duties derived from our image of the ideal. Indeed some of us can already feel the weight of that chain around our necks.[132] Let me make a few preliminary comments so that I may have fewer apprehensions about presenting the formula that summarizes the new circle of duties that we have been speaking about.

[34] Deeper human beings have at all times felt compassion with the animals because they suffer from life without having

any power to turn the sting against themselves and to understand their own existence metaphysically. To witness such pointless suffering is profoundly appalling. Thus the suspicion arose, in several places around the world, that the burdened souls of guilty human beings had become embodied in these animals, and that what looks so appalling at first glance turns out, before the eye of eternal justice, to be full of good sense and meaning, as punishment and penance. It is truly a grave punishment to live as an animal, driven by hunger and craving, unable to arrive at any comprehension of life. What worse fate could there be than that of a beast of prey chased through the wild by its own gnawing torments, denied all but the most fleeting satisfactions, {377/378} which soon turn into agony, as it runs from one deadly fight to another, beset by disgusting greed and doomed to nausea from mindlessly gorging itself whenever it can? To cling so blindly and madly to a worthless life, far from any awareness that one is being punished, let alone for what, and indeed to lust for that very punishment as if it were happiness, with the utter stupidity of the most savage craving — that is what it means to be an animal. If the whole of nature presses on towards Man,[133] it goes to show how desperately she needs to be redeemed from the curse of animal life and that with man existence has finally arrived at a mirror in whose reflections life may no longer appear meaningless, but rather imbued with metaphysical significance at last. Let us consider, then, where the animal ends and where man truly begins — that Man in whom nature is so exclusively interested! He who craves life as if it were a pleasure has not raised his sight above the animal horizon; he only desires with a measure of awareness what the animal seeks blindly. But so it goes with most of us most of the time: we cannot usually escape animal existence, and thus we are ourselves those animals that appear to be suffering so meaninglessly.

[35a] Then there are moments *when we understand*, when the clouds are scattered and we can see ourselves, along with

everything else in nature, pressing on towards Man, towards something high above us.[134] We look around in the sudden light and shudder at what we see: there go the refined beasts of prey, and we among them. The immense mobility of human beings in their vast worldly wilderness; their countless cities and states; their perennial warfare; their ceaseless gathering and scattering; their hustling and bustling; their mutual imitation; their tripping one another up and trampling one another down; their wailing in distress and their howling in triumph — all of it is just a continuation of animal life, as if man were to be deliberately reduced again and cheated out of his metaphysical endowments, as if nature, after yearning for {378/379} and working towards man for so long, were now shrinking from him and wished to return to the unconscious life of instinct. Alas, nature needs insight but dreads it at the same time, however great her need; and so the flame flickers to and fro, restless and almost afraid of itself, touching on a thousand things before finally settling on that which needed illumination in the first place.

[35b] There are occasional moments when we all realize that our most elaborate arrangements are made because we wish to escape our essential task in life; that we are eager to hide our heads in the sand, as if our hundred-eyed[135] conscience were unable to find us out; that we quickly give our hearts away to the state, to money-making, to social life, or to science, only so that we may be rid of it; that we go much further than our livelihood would require in enslaving ourselves to the most wearisome drudgery, because nothing seems more necessary to us than to keep ourselves from gaining consciousness. We are all in a rush because we are all running from ourselves; we are all bashfully eager to disguise our hurry because we would like to seem happy and to fool any keen-sighted observers who might discover our actual misery; and we all feel the need for ever-new tinkling-cymbal-words[136] that we might use to embellish life and give it a festive appearance. We all know how peculiar a state it puts us in when unwelcome memories suddenly force

themselves upon us and how we do everything we can to chase them from our minds with a flurry of activity and as much clatter as possible. So it is evident from the noisy activity of everyday life that we are in such a state all the time, terrified of memory and the inward life. What is it that keeps assailing us, what mosquito is robbing us of sleep? Every moment of life wants to tell us something; it is as if we were surrounded by ghosts whose voices we do not want to hear. We get afraid that when we are alone and quiet something might be whispered in our ears, and so we hate the silence and numb ourselves with socializing. {**379/380**}

[36] Now and then we do understand and get puzzled by our own vertiginous fear and haste, by the whole sleep-walking condition in which we so dread awakening and dream all the more vividly and restlessly as morning nears. We also feel, however, that we are too weak to endure such inner awareness for more than a moment and that we are not those men towards whom nature is pressing. It is already a lot for us that we occasionally lift our heads a little above the water and that we notice how deeply we are submerged in the stream. Even when we do surface and awaken for a fleeting moment, our own strength does not suffice for us, but we need helpers to lift us up — and who are those helpers?

[37a] They are the true men, those who are animals no more: *the philosophers, artists, and saints.* At their emergence, by their emergence, nature jumps for joy, just that once, although she never takes any leaps otherwise.[137] For the first time nature senses that she has attained her end, whereupon she realizes that she must wean herself from having goals and that she has carried the game of life and becoming too far. She is transfigured by her realization and her face is illumined by the mild fatigue of the evening, by "beauty," as human beings call it. What her radiant features now reveal is the great *enlightenment*[138] about existence, and the highest wish that any mortal can make is for his eyes and ears to be opened so that he might share in

this enlightenment permanently. When one considers all the things that Schopenhauer must have *heard* in his life, will one not cry out, "How deaf are my ears! How dull is my mind, how flickering my reason, how shrunken my heart! Alas, how contemptible is all that I call my own. What misery to flap one's wings without being able to fly; to see something high above oneself without being able to rise; {380/381} to arrive at the path towards which the unfathomably free gaze of the philosopher points, and to take a few stumbling steps, only to turn immediately back."

[37b] If one's highest wish were to come true even for a *single* day, how gladly one would pay for it with all the rest of one's life! The soul becomes solitary and boundless when one so much as imagines oneself climbing up to the highest peaks of thought, where the air is purest and coldest, where there is an end to mists and veils, where things communicate their innermost properties in a language that is rough and rigid, but unmistakably clear. Let the soul's wish come true, let a man's gaze rest even once upon things with the straightness and brightness of a beam of light — and it would be the end of all shame, all fear, and all craving. What words could do justice to such a state of unprecedented, mysterious alertness without agitation, the state of a soul like Schopenhauer's when it expands itself upon the immense hieroglyphics of existence, upon the principles of becoming inscribed upon every stone, not blanketing everything with the dark of night, but rather flooding the world with the gleaming rays of rose-fingered dawn.[139] What could be more miserable, on the other hand, than the lot of the less-gifted man who has glimpsed just enough of the unique destiny and bliss of the philosopher to feel how arbitrary and unfulfilled is his own life — that of the non-philosopher — whose desires are as vain as they are hopeless, and who knows that he is a fruit off the same tree, only trapped in the shade where he can never ripen, even as he sees the sunlight reach the branches just beside his!

[38] These torments might easily make the less-gifted man

envious and spiteful, if he were made of such stuff; but in the end, he is likely to turn around his soul so that it might no longer be consumed by yearning, and that is when he will *discover a new circle of duties.*

[39a] Now I am ready to answer the question whether it is possible to draw close to the great ideal of Schopenhauerian man by one's own regular activity. One thing above all is certain: the new duties of which we are speaking are not {381/382} meant to isolate a man, but rather to give him a place within a powerful communion of purpose, a purpose that is not defined by external forms or laws, but by a central idea, the idea of *culture*, which challenges every one of us with the single-minded demand *that we should contribute our share to the perfection of nature, both within ourselves and outside ourselves, that is, to the emergence of the philosopher, the artist, and the saint.* For just as nature needs the philosopher, so she needs the artist for a metaphysical end: so that she might become enlightened about herself, so that she might finally see in pure and perfected form what she never gets to see owing to the restlessness of her own becoming; in other words, that she might become self-aware. It was Goethe who expressed in exuberant and profound words how all nature's efforts are directed towards the artist who can guess what she means by her mumbling, who can meet her half-way and can express her real intentions: "I have said it many time before," Goethe exclaims, "and I will keep repeating it: the final end of all the world's business, and of man within it, is dramatic poetry. The stuff of life is good for nothing else."[140]

[39b] Finally, nature needs the saint whose ego has melted away entirely and whose passions and sufferings in life are no longer felt in separation from other beings, but rather give rise to the most profound sense of communion, compassion, and oneness with all living things. In the saint we see the miracle of transformation that is so exceptional in the game of becoming, that final and ultimate attainment of Manhood[141] towards which nature presses and pushes as towards her own redemption. No

doubt we are all related and connected to the saint, as we are all related to the philosopher and the artist. There are moments — sparks from the brightest fires of loving-kindness, we might say — in whose light we no longer understand the word "I"; {382/383} for there is something on the other side of our being to which we gain access in those special moments, something that leaves us yearning from the bottom of our hearts for the bridges whereby we might keep crossing from here to there.

[39c] In our usual condition, on the other hand, we have little to contribute to the emergence of the redeeming man; that is why we *loathe* ourselves in that condition, a loathing that is at the root of the pessimism with which Schopenhauer reacquainted our age, though it is as old as is the yearning for culture. I call loathing the root, not the flower of that pessimism; its ground-floor, not its steeple; the starting point of its journey, not the destination. For there will come a time when we will need to learn a different kind of hatred, aimed at a much more general object than our individuality and its wretched limitations, its transience and restlessness; a time when we will attain a higher condition that will also teach us to love something other than what we are able to love now. Once we have ourselves been admitted, in this life or another, to the holy orders of the philosopher, the artist, and the saint, a new direction will be given to our love and our hatred; in the meantime, we have been given our task and our circle of duties, our hatred and our love, as we can know them now.

[39d] We understand what culture requires. She demands that we apply the ideal of Schopenhauerian man practically by preparing and promoting his emergence in ever-novel ways, by getting to know what stands in the way and removing it. In short, she wants us to fight relentlessly against anything that might deprive *us* of the highest fulfillment of our existence by preventing us from becoming Schopenhauerian men ourselves.[142]

NOTES

1. Or miracle.

2. Nietzsche's challenge will stand, as a final summation, at the head of his last completed work, *Ecce Homo: How One Becomes What One Is* (1888). It looks back to the famous Delphic inscription, of course (γνῶθι σαυτόν), but likewise ahead (with some qualifications) to much contemporary therapeutic and spiritual literature, the books of Eckart Tolle, for instance. (See especially par. 31 {374-75}.) As an Eastern master might say: "When you become you, Zen becomes Zen." Or even: "Kill the Buddha!" (Compare Shunryu Suzuki, *Zen Mind, Beginner's Mind* (Boston: Shambhala, 2011), pp. 9, 68, 71.) Thus also *Zarathustra*: "For that is what I am through and through: ... a raiser, cultivator, and disciplinarian, who once counseled himself, not for nothing: 'Become who you are!'" (Kaufmann IV.239; KSA 4.297)

3. G: *Scheinmenschen*: those who merely appear or pretend to be men.

4. See par. 23 {364}.

5. Heraclitus made much of the river as a symbol for the transient nature of all things in the universe. All things are in flux (Πάντα ῥεῖ), and nothing ever remains still; no man steps into the same river twice; we are and we are not. See also par. 18

{358} and my note on the image of the river in various Indian traditions.

6. Even the greatest insights and philosophical systems, writes Nietzsche, can only be entirely true (if ever) for their discoverers and founders themselves (PtZG, Preface: KSA 1.801).

7. Compare *Zarathustra*: "'This is *my* way; where is yours?' — thus I answered those who asked me 'the way.' For *the* way — that does not exist." (Kaufmann III.195; KSA 4.245)

8. Oliver Cromwell, as quoted by Pomponne de Bellièvre to Cardinal de Retz in 1651 (*Memoirs of Cardinal de Retz* [1717]). The Cardinal made an equally memorable reply: "'You know, monsieur,' said I to Bellièvre, 'that I abhor Cromwell; and whatever is commonly reported of his great parts, if he is of this opinion, I must pronounce him a fool.'" Nietzsche had read Cromwell's pronouncement in a German translation of Emerson's essay on "Circles" and underlined it multiple times (KSA 14.74-75 [*Kommentar*]).

9. See par. 31 {374}.

10. G: *Erzieher und Bildner*. The German *Erziehung* can imply schooling and discipline (thus also the somewhat archaic term *Zucht* (for strict discipline), which is derived from the same root *ziehen*, to draw or pull: a little further down Nietzsche will speak of Schopenhauer as a *Zuchtmeister*). *Erzieher*, not unlike the English *educator* (related to L *educere*: to lead forth), suggests someone who does not merely convey knowledge, but rather draws or leads another out of ignorance. (See also Nietzsche's reference to Schopenhauer as a *Führer*, a guide or leader in par. 17 {356}.) The nuances of *Bildung* are notoriously difficult to replicate in English. The verb *bilden* (from *Bild*: a picture) means to form (as after an image), and *Bildung* tends much more strongly than its English counterparts to imply high culture, artistic creativity, and aspiration to an ideal (as in the German term for fine arts: *bildende Künste*).

11. G: *Ursinn*.

12. G: *Bildung.*

13. G: *Afterbild der Erziehung.*

14. The adjective *trüb(e)* refers to the quality of opaqueness, dullness, or murkiness in liquids that are not clear. So Nietzsche's cloud is thick and impenetrable. But the word is also used more loosely, speaking of eyes or moods or the weather, for instance, and *Trübsal* refers to a state or grief or gloom, often with a mocking note: thus *Trübsal blasen*, or moping.

15. As above: *Erzieher und Bildner.*

16. G: *Lehrer und Zuchtmeister.*

17. Nietzsche writes *Kräfte und Säfte*, as in the forces and fluids that give a tree its strength. The image was a favorite of Herder's, for one, but here it has the ring of cliché and perhaps irony.

18. Benvenuto Cellini (1500-1571) was an Italian goldsmith and many-sided Renaissance man who wrote a famous biography. His musician father had sought without success to dissuade him from metalwork in his youth. Despite his early distaste for music-making, Cellini fils became a celebrated flutist.

19. One is reminded of the young Mozart, who had a similarly overbearing father and a like distaste for playing the flute. Cellini reports in his *Autobiography* that while his father made and loved all manner of "little pipes," he himself had "an inexpressible dislike" for the instrument from the earliest days of his childhood (ch. 5). Thus also ch. 11: "My father ... kept writing piteous entreaties ... and in every letter bade me not to lose the music he had taught me with such trouble. Thus I lost all desire to return to him, *so much did I hate that accursed music.*" (Italics added) In chapter 24 he even speaks of his *enslavement* to that accursed art.

20. Of the pre-Socratic philosophers he admired especially — Heraclitus, Pythagoras, and Empedocles — Nietzsche says the following at KSA 1.757-58 (*Fünf Vorreden: Über das Pathos der Wahrheit*): "It is important to discover that there once lived

such men. As a mere idle possibility, one would never imagine the pride of the wise Heraclitus, for example. The striving for knowledge as such, by its very nature, must always seem incomplete and unsatisfactory; and so nobody would believe, if he were not otherwise instructed by history, that such a royal self-confidence, such an unbounded conviction that one is the only blessed suitor of truth, could really exist. Such men live in their own solar system, and that is where one must seek them out." At KSA 1.809 (PtZG 1) Nietzsche writes that a real philosopher will be, in the best case, "the greatest star in the solar system of culture," but where he is not bound to any true culture, "an unpredictable and therefore terrifying comet." (See also the next note.)

21. Compare KSA 1.807-808 (PtZG 1): "Any people must be ashamed when it is reminded of so miraculous and ideal a society of philosophers as that of the ancient Greek masters Thales, Anaximander, Heraclitus, Parmenides, Anaxagoras, Empedocles, Democritus, and Socrates. All these men are wholly hewn from one stone... Together, they form what Schopenhauer called a republic of geniuses, in contrast to a republic of mere scholars (*Gelehrtenrepublik*). One giant calls out to the other across the barren intervals of time, and the dialogue persists unbothered by the obstinate clamoring and creeping of the pygmies."

22. Nietzsche's disgust with tin-eared and impenetrable German writing will come as no surprise to anyone who has been exposed to the ways of the German academy. "Everything ponderous, torpid, and ceremoniously gawky, all wordy and tedious manners of style are developed among the Germans in the most proliferating diversity," he writes in section 28 of *Jenseits von Gut und Böse* (KSA 5.46). Thus also section 246: "What torture are books written in German for anyone who has a third ear! How unwillingly such a man will stand beside the slowly revolving morass of sounds without sound and rhythms

without dance that passes for a 'book' among Germans." (KSA 5.189) Nietzsche admired Goethe, placing him in proximity to Schopenhauer (see par. 11b {347}) and also among his own "ancestors," alongside Heraclitus, Empedocles, and Spinoza (*Nachlaß*: KSA 11.134, see also 11.150); but all this is for his personal stature and his celebrated plays and poems, not for his "stiff and prissy Rococo prose style" (KSA 5.46). For more on Goethe and Lessing, see par. 11b {347-48}. Heine, in Nietzsche's view, is a stylistic virtuoso who delights too much in playing the motley fool [*er liebt die bunte Hanswurstjacke*], while Hegel's pen turns everything to gray (*Nachlaß*: KSA 281).

23. The *gymnasium* (from γυμνάζω, to train naked) was where the ancient Greeks gathered for physical exercise and intellectual exchange. German preserves the memory of the latter in the name of those secondary schools that confer the *Abitur* and are meant to prepare students for the university. Naked exercises are no longer customary.

24. Nietzsche's *Schar* could be composed of men or beasts, though the image of sheep being herded off to the slaughter suggests itself strongly enough here (Jer. 11:19, 53:7; Isa. 53:6-7).

25. Nietzsche's use of *Höcker* suggests not only physically and mentally hunched-over creatures, but camel-like beasts of burden roaming a barren desert. In Zarathustra, the camel appears both as a mere beast to be loaded (Kaufmann III.193, KSA 4.243) and as representing a crucial stage of spiritual transformation (Kaufmann I.25-27; KSA 4.29-31).

26. Nietzsche is playing on the contrast between the good and the better in a way I am not able to replicate very well here; but see just below.

27. Thus the French saying *Le mieux est l'ennemi du bien* (better is the enemy of good), which Schopenhauer cites with approval in his *Aphorismen* (ch. 5, p. 154).

28. In *Ecce Homo*, surveying his lifetime's work, Nietzsche

concluded that "what led [him] to Schopenhauer was *atheism*" (KSA 6.318).

29. Schopenhauer required no less of his readers: "I demand of anyone who wishes to acquaint himself with my philosophy that he read every line of mine." (*Die Welt as Wille und Vorstellung*, 2 vols. in 1, edited by Ludger Lütkehaus [Munich: DTV, 1998] 2.40.535 [herafter *WWV*, cited by volume, section, and page number])

30. Schopenhauer published the first edition of his *Welt als Wille und Vorstellung* when he was thirty years old, in 1818-19, and kept refining the work all his life, publishing a second and third edition in 1844 and 1859, respectively. Nietzsche stumbled upon a first edition in a local bookstore when he was 21 years old, in 1865.

31. More literally, Schopenhauer never wishes to *seem* (*scheinen*). Karl Friedrich Schinkel (1781 - 1841), the great Prussian architect, had declared in 1832: "I consider it a dereliction of duty to wish to seem more than I am." Contrast the equally duty-minded Immanuel Kant (par. 14 {351}), who in Nietzsche's view made a point of maintaining religious appearances, among other opportunistic accommodations.

32. It is this vision of Schopenhauer's life as "guided by the motto *vitam impendere vero* [to risk one's life for the truth]" (section 7, {411}) that so inspired Nietzsche. (In a lengthy note to section XI of his Letter to d'Alembert, Rousseau claims the same motto for himself [Bloom translation p. 132].)

33. Zarathustra is likened to a bear in Book II (Kaufmann II.145; KSA 4.187).

34. Thus it is Lessing, rather than Goethe, who stands as the exception in German literature according to Nietzsche, "thanks to his actor's nature, which understood much and was capable of much" (*Jenseits von Gut und Böse*: KSA 5.46).

35. Montaigne's admiration for Plutarch was boundless: "If [Jacques Amyot's French translation of Plutarch's *Lives*] had

not raised us [modern] ignoramuses out of the dirt, we would have been lost." (*Essays* II.iv) But Nietzsche misrepresents what Montaigne said about the leg and the wing (*Essays* III.v). Montaigne was actually worried about being charged with "pillage" because helped himself to bits from Plutarch on so many occasions.

36. G: *erheiternde Heiterkeit*. I will be translating *Heiterkeit* as cheerfulness, *Fröhlichkeit* as joyfulness. Normally *erheiternd* means amusing in German, so Nietzsche is also drawing attention to how funny Schopenhauer can be in the original, though usually in a rather cutting way.

37. Emerson invokes the Latin proverb in part 7 of his *Conduct of Life*: "It is an old commendation of right behavior, '*Aliis laetus, sapiens sibi*,' which our English proverb translates, 'Be merry and wise.' (...) I know those miserable fellows, and I hate them, who see a black star always riding through the light and colored clouds in the sky overhead: waves of light pass over and hide it for a moment, but the black star keeps fast in the zenith. But power dwells with cheerfulness; hope puts us in a working mood, whilst despair is no muse, and untunes the active powers. A man should make life and Nature happier to us, or he had better never been born."

38. Thus Alfred Baeumler, in his Afterword to the 1930 Kröner edition of the *Unzeitgemäße Betrachtungen*, "What Nietzsche admires about Schopenhauer is the fearless forthrightness of his gaze and his expressions. He sees in him as one of Dürer's knight's fighting his way through death and damnation."

39. It should be borne in mind that by the common teaching of mankind's greatest sages, it is he who conquers *himself* that is the greatest victor, not he who subdues hosts of external enemies. Thus the *Dhammapada*, verse 103, for example: "Greater than to conquer a thousand times a thousand men in battle it is to conquer oneself," which is echoed in nearly identical terms by Jain ("Though a man should conquer thousands and thousands

of valiant foes, greater will be his victory if he conquers nobody but himself." [*Uttaradhyayana Sutra* 9.34]); by Rumi: "The lion who breaks the enemy's ranks is a minor hero compared to the lion who overcomes himself."; in the Tao Te Ching, ch. 33; in Proverbs 16:32; and in countless other credible sources besides.

40. The subject of Nietzsche's rather ungenerous First Meditation: "David Strauß, der Bekenner und der Schriftsteller." In *Ecce Homo*, Nietzsche reaffirms that he had set out upon a "war" or an "assassination attempt," driven by "merciless contempt" for what he took Strauß to represent (KSA 6.316-17).

41. G: *seiend.* The passage is from Goethe's *Tagebuch der italienischen Reise* IV, 9 Oct. 1786 (*Kommentar:* KSA 14.76).

42. G: *Naturgewächs*, suggesting gradual organic growth, not sudden creation.

43. A mystical Greek creature, half-goat and half-stag.

44. Schopenhauer had died in 1860, five years before Nietzsche's discovery.

45. Nietzsche discerns a whiff of "the intoxicating, dark scent of things Indian" about Pythagoras and Empedocles (PtZG 11: KSA 1.845). At KSA 1.806 (PtZG 1), Nietzsche observes that "nothing would be more foolish than to speak of the Greeks as if their education had been autonomous (*autochthon*); they rather drank up whatever living knowledge they could find among all the other peoples, and they got as far as they did precisely because they knew to throw the spear from where another people had dropped it. What is so admirable about them is their art of learning fruitfully; and so, like them, we ought to learn from our neighbors — with life as our end, not academic knowledge — using what we learn as a prop by means of which we might soar above and beyond them."

46. Lest Kant's servility be doubted (compare also {414}), suffice it to recall that his missives to King Frederick William II were signed with the phrase "I mortify myself in utmost

devotion as your Eternal Majesty's most abject slave [*Knecht*]."

47. In section 7, Nietzsche makes a hard distinction between the scholar (*Gelehrter*) and the true philosopher and insists that Kant, for all his genius, never passed from the "cocoon stage" to true philosophy {409}. A philosopher, after all, is "not just a great thinker, but a full human being, and what scholar could claim as much for himself?" {409-10} In *Ecce Homo*, Nietzsche likewise stresses how far (*meilenweit!*) he wishes to distance his own concept of "a philosopher" from a conception "that would even include a Kant, not to mention the academic 'masticators' and other professors of philosophy" (KSA 6.320).

48. The passage is from chapter 4 (Nation-Making) of Walter Bagehot's *Physics and Politics* (1872). A sentence from ch. 3 is even more topical: "It is the life of teachers which is catching, not their tenets." The German text is corrupted and denies that Shelley could have lived in *England*!

49. The German poets Friedrich Hölderlin (1770-1843) and Heinrich von Kleist (1777-1811).

50. G: *Bildung*. Thus Nietzsche's diatribe against German cultural complacency (and against David Strauß, whom he takes to be its incarnation) in the First Meditation. Nietzsche reaffirms his utter contempt (*schonungslose Verachtung*) for German *Bildung* in *Ecce Homo*: KSA 6.316-19.

51. To be precise, *erzen*, that is, made from (iron) ore. Nietzsche may have wished to avoid speaking of *Eisen* in order to keep his distance from the blood-and-iron rhetoric of Bismarck and his devotees. It was in his address of 30 Sep. 1862 before the Prussian legislature that Bismarck declared that "the great questions of the day," those surrounding German unification, would be decided "by blood and iron." Nietzsche's contempt for that kind of talk is paraded with remarkable freedom, not to say abandon, in his First Meditation.

52. That is, a struggle full of tensions or even convulsions. Nietzsche's *Kampf und Krampf* is a common play on the similarity

between the German words for a fight or struggle (*Kampf*) and for a cramp (*Krampf*), thus emphasizing the indignities rather than the glories of fighting.

53. Goethe adds that he is not just translating the French, but rendering it in the manner in which "an alert, straight German" might have put it. The anecdote, and the following passage, is taken from Goethe's essay "Antik und modern" (J.W. von Goethe, *Kunsttheoretische Schriften und Übersetzungen* (Berliner Ausgabe), vol. 20, ed. by S. Seidel [Berlin: Aufbau, 1960 ff.])

54. This from the very Goethe who is said to have moved Napoleon to exclaim, "There's a *man!*" ("*Voilà un homme!*") — roughly that *Ecce homo!* which Nietzsche places at the head of his last, summarizing work, and which he would surely have welcomed as his own epitaph. Pilate, whose *ecce homo* in the Vulgate translation of John 19:5 gave rise to the expression, was for Nietzsche "the only figure in the New Testament worth honoring" (*Antichrist*, par. 46).

55. G: *Bildungsphilister*. Nietzsche prided himself on having coined this term (in his First Meditation) and on having left it as his permanent bequest to the German language (*Ecce Homo*: KSA 6.317). Walter Kaufmann points out, in a footnote to the passage in his own translation, that the word had been used earlier by Gustav Teichmüller (1832-88), a professor at Basel around the time that Nietzsche wrote his Meditations.

56. *The World as Will and Representation* (1818), compare KSA 1.811. In 1835, Schopenhauer's publisher, Brockhaus, sent the following note: "I regret to inform you that I am feeling compelled to pulp most of the remaining stock of your work so that I might derive at least a small benefit from it."

57. Compare *WWV*, 2.40.535: "I write as the ancients did, with no other intention than to put my thoughts on record so that they might one day benefit those who are capable of valuing and reflecting upon them properly."

58. On occasions when the dog had misbehaved, Schopenhauer

was in the habit of scolding him by calling him "human."

59. In *Beyond Good and Evil*, section 204, Nietzsche praises Heraclitus, Plato, and Empedocles as "royal and magnificent recluses of the spirit" (KSA 5.131). Thus also "magnificent loneliness" at KSA 1.807.

60. G: *Ichts und Nichts*. It was the German mystic Jakob Böhme (1575-1624) who came up with the term "Ichts" as an alternative to "ich" (I) that would express what he saw as the perfect opposition between I-ness and Nothing ("Nichts"). Thus: "Heaven and hell are as distant as day and night, as *Ichts* and *Nichts*." Hegel called Böhme "the first German philosopher" and discussed his conception of *Ichts* in his *Lectures on the History of Philosophy* (*Vorlesungen über die Geschichte der Philosophie*, edited by C. L. Michelet, being vol. 15 of Hegel's *Werke*, Second edition [Berlin: Duncker und Humblot, 1844], pp. 286-87 [Part 3, Section 1B]).

61. Kleist killed himself, at the age of 34, on 21 Nov. 1811, but the construction that Nietzsche puts on his death is rather implausible. In a letter to Marie von Kleist (17 Sep. 1811), an older friend and distant relation, Kleist summarizes his mood in the final months of his life: "My soul feels altogether numbed and dulled and I do not see a single bright point in the future to which I might look forward with joy and hope... It is odd how everything that I undertake these days seems to miscarry, and how every time I resolve to take a firm step, the rug is pulled out from under my feet." Far from hinting at feelings of being unloved, however, he asks Marie, "Just how have I deserved to get so much love from you?" Less than two weeks before his death, he reports on his resolve to die: "I swear that it has become impossible for me to continue living. My soul is so sore that I cannot stick my nose out the window without being hurt by the sunlight... All the beauty and decency I have know in life ... has left me so sensitive that even the smallest and most ordinary upsets injure me twice or three times over."

(To Marie von Kleist, 10 Nov. 1811) What dooms Kleist is a morbid attraction to Henriette Vogel, a terminally ill-friend, with whom he enters into a suicide pact. On the day of his death he condemns his own life as "the most torturous that ever a man has led," but his exit from it as "the most magnificent and voluptuous of all deaths." (To Marie von Kleist, 21 Nov. 1811) In a farewell-note to his half-sister Ulrike, he professes himself "content and joyful and at peace with all the world" and adds: "Truly, you have done everything within the power of a sister, nay of a human being, to save me. The truth is that there was nothing to be done for me on this earth." (To Ulrike von Kleist, 21 Nov. 1811) In his notes to himself, Nietzsche offers the more convincing diagnosis that "the noble Kleist" may have been doomed by an excess of thought and a lack of Schopenhauerian philosophy (*Nachlaß*: KSA 7.712 [29(204)]; 7.723 [29(230)]; 13.249 [14(63)] and 13.502 [16(48)]).

62. Not just *siegend*, but *siegreich*, lit. rich in victory. Compare par. 12 {348-49}.

63. He being one of the iron natures in par. 16a {352}.

64. The morbid tendency of philosophers to degenerate into mere thought-machines is traced back to the early example of Parmenides at KSA 1.836 (PtZG 9).

65. Thus Kleist's letters of 22 and 23 March 1801 — nearly identical with respect to the above passages about Kant — to his then-fiancé Wilhelmine von Zenge and to his half-sister Ulrike von Kleist, respectively. In both letters, but especially the second, Kleist professes himself so overwhelmed by agitation and disgust that he fears for his sanity. Nietzsche appears to have taken the "most devastatingly moving (*erschütterndst*)" quality of Kleist's letters very much to heart (*Kommentar*: KSA 14.76).

66. A nod, surely, at Kant's famous phrase from the *Grundlegung zur Metaphysik der Sitten* (1785): "the starry heavens above me and the moral law within me."

67. The German *Stricke* does rather suggest the kind of rope one might hang oneself with.

68. That is, not even half-philosophies, but half of the half, perhaps with a nod at drawing and quartering (compare {424}).

69. Nietzsche writes *seines Wollens*, not *seines Willens*, so the word will is better avoided here. The particular flavor of *sittlich* would present difficulties even if the line between ethics and morals ran more clearly in English.

70. Nietzsche stresses that his attacks on Christianity must by no means be applied to Buddhism, which he finds to be "a hundred times more realistic" and indeed "the only really *positivistic* religion in history." (Thus also *Morgenröte*, section 96: "There appeared the teacher of a religion of self-liberation, the Buddha: how far Europe still is from that stage of culture!" [KSA 3.87]) He understands the Buddha as a profound therapist and "physiologist" who has advanced "*beyond* good and evil," much like Nietzsche himself, and his main objection to the Buddha's "touching" teaching is its supposedly nihilistic and decadent orientation (*Antichrist*: KSA 6.186-87; *Ecce Homo*: KSA 6.273). In *Beyond Good and Evil*, section 56, Nietzsche pairs the Buddha with Schopenhauer and claims to have outdone them both by plumbing the depths of world-negation "with an Asian, and more than an Asian eye." (KSA 5.74) Perhaps Nietzsche would have been more sympathetic still if he had been more aware that joyful acceptance rather than negation is at the heart of the Buddha's teaching and that any craving for annihilation (or rebirth!) is a grave impediment to liberation. That craving is indeed the root of culture (even of life itself) is a central tenet in Buddhism, but with much more devastating implications than Nietzsche realizes.

71. G: *ein siegreich Vollendeter.*

72. On Rancé, though not the anecdote, see *WWV*, 2.48.733.

73. See par. 3 {340}. The image of river-crossing as a representation of the spiritual quest recurs frequently in

all Indian traditions: thus in Buddhism (see for instance *Dhammapada* 85), in the *Bhagavad Gita* (4.36) and in the Hindu Vedas more generally, as well as in the Jain and Sikh scriptures.

74. A line from Faust's famous opening monologue, in which he explains why, having wearied of life, he has finally turned to magic:

> Mich plagen keine Skrupel noch Zweifel,
> Fürchte mich weder vor Hölle noch Teufel –
> Dafür ist mir auch alle Freud' entrissen,
> Bilde mir nicht ein was rechts zu wissen,
> Bilde mir nicht ein, ich könnte was lehren,
> Die Menschen zu bessern und zu bekehren.
> Auch hab' ich weder Gut noch Geld,
> Noch Ehr' und Herrlichkeit der Welt.
> *Es möchte kein Hund so länger leben!*
> Drum hab' ich mich der Magie ergeben."

Which in a younger man's somewhat free translation might read:

> I know not scruple's pang or doubt,
> Fear neither spell nor Satan's clout —
> Yet life is void of joy or pleasure
> Of honor, glory, earthly treasure.
> I don't presume to know what's right
> To show my fellow man the light;
> Improve man's lot or teach him well,
> I could not do it, life is hell.
> And since no dog could bear such squalor,
> I've taken loans in magic's dollar.

75. The word lava does not appear here, but it is implied in Nietzsche's *erkaltet* that the rock was once molten and moving.

76. Compare Zarathustra: "[W]oe unto all the living that would live without disputes over weight and scales and

weighers." (Kaufmann II.117; KSA 4.151)

77. G: *Zwiespalt.*

78. G: *Trieb.*

79. See par. 22 {363}. Nietzsche traces this question back to Thales, "the great model for Empedocles" (see just below).

80. Compare par. 22 {363}. Nietzsche was inclined to consider Empedocles "the perfect Greek [*der ideal-vollkommene Grieche*]" (*Nachlaß*: KSA 7.83) and included him among the "ancestors" mentioned above (*Nachlaß*: KSA 11.134). "With *Empedocles and Democritus*, the Greeks were well on their way towards giving a proper estimate of human existence, its unreason, its suffering; but they never got there. Thanks to Socrates." (*Nachlaß*: KSA 8.107, italics added) Nietzsche permitted himself the hope that a "resurrection" of their thought might be under way (*Nachlaß*: KSA 11.442): "Every day we are getting more *Greek*: first, as is only proper, in our concepts and evaluations, in the manner of Hellenizing ghosts; but eventually, let us hope, with out very *bodies*. Therein lies my hope for the German soul [*Wesen*] (and therein it has always lain)." (*Nachlaß*: KSA 11.679)

What Nietzsche sees in Empedocles is specifically an affirmation of life in its joyfully struggling, *agonistic* dimension (*Nachlaß*: KSA 7.399, 7.524, 7.547), the embrace of the instincts (*Nachlaß*: 7.154, 7. 249, 7.462) and of all that is "deeply irrational even within that which is most rational [*das tief Unvernuenftige im Vernuenftigsten der Welt*]" (*Nachlaß*: 8.106). The special affinity between Empedocles and Schopenhauer is stressed in section 4 of the Fourth Untimely Meditation (*Wagner in Bayreuth*): "Between Schopenhauer and Empedocles ... there are such similarities and affinities that one is almost physically struck by the very relative nature of all concept of time [*das sehr relative Wesen aller Zeitbegriffe*]. One might think that some things belong together and time is merely a cloud that makes it difficult for our eyes to see the connection." (KSA 1.446)

Nietzsche was familiar with Diogenes Laërtius' biographical

sketch (*The Lives and Opinions of Eminent Philosophers*, translated by C.D. Young [London: Henry G. Bohn, 1853], pp. 359-69), but as later with the figure of Zarathustra, he freely adapts the historical legend to his ends. In the first extant lines of Empedocles' "wonderful poem" (KSA 1.811), Empedocles appears to declare himself divine, at least in relation to his contemporaries: "I go about among you an immortal god, honored by all." (Fragment 112 [Diehls], DL 364) Further on, Empedocles claims that he could easily see, with his mind's eye, "all the things that are in ten or twenty human lifetimes" (Diehls 129). Diogenes Laërtius quotes him, to similar effect, with the words: "For once I was a boy, and once a girl, a bush, a bird, a fish who swims the sea." (DL 368, Diehls 117) In the idea of a circular transmigration of souls (DL 339-41), which Empedocles seems to have learned from Pythagoras before being expelled from his school for divulging secret doctrines (DL 360), Nietzsche heard echoes of his own conception of eternal recurrence. (KSA 1.758 refers to "the great conception of the soul's transmigration and the unity of all beings." [*Fünf Vorreden: Über das Pathos der Wahrheit*])

In an early letter to a friend, dated 19 Oct. 1861, when he had just turned seventeen, Nietzsche embraced the treatment of the legend by his "favorite poet", Friedrich Hölderlin: "In his uncompleted tragedy 'Empedocles' [*Der Tod des Empedokles*] the poet reveals his own nature to us. Empedocles' death is a death out of divine pride, out of disdain for men, from earth-satiety and pantheism. The whole work has moved me exceedingly whenever I've read it; there is a divine majesty about this Empedocles." ("Mein Lebenslauf (III)" in Friedrich Nietzsche, *Werke* [Munich, 1954], vol. 3, pp. 96-97) A decade later, in the fall of 1870, Nietzsche produced the beginnings of his own drama about Empedocles, in which the hero is associated to Dionysius and proclaims the truth of reincarnation, and where the famous phrase from *Zarathustra* — "God is dead" — is anticipated in the line "The Great Plan is dead!" The legendary end of Empedocles' life, with a leap into the abyss of an active volcano, must have resonated particularly with Nietzsche. (See *Nachlaß*: KSA 7.125-26, 233-37.)

81. Compare Nietzsche's *Reich der verklärten Physis* in par. 22b {363}.

82. G: *das echte Kind seiner Zeit.*

83. Whereas Nietzsche writes *Kind seiner Zeit* (the child of *his* age or times) at the outset of the paragraph, now he switches to *Kind der Zeit* (child of time). In the next sentence, too, the (step-) mother is not *seine Zeit* (his age or times), but *die Zeit*, that is, time in general.

84. Nietzsche reads Schopenhauer as having recognized, like Heraclitus, "that the past and the future are as unreal as a dream, while the present is merely the spaceless, insubstantial divide between the two, so that time, like space, and likewise anything that has its being in space and time, exists only in a relative sense." (PtZG 5: KSA 1.823-24) See also the quotation about time being "merely a cloud" in the long footnote note on Empedocles (KSA 1.446).

85. G: *sein Wesen* (also in par. 22b).

86. G: *(das Reich) der verklärten Physis* (also in par. 21 {362}).

87. A characteristically Greek question, Nietzsche believes (see par. 21b {361}), which Schopenhauer answers with unrivaled ruthlessness in his chapter on "The Nullity and Misery of Human Life" (*WWV* 2.46.665-684).

88. G: *zeitgemäß* (see note on *die Zeit*, par. 22 {362-63}).

89. G: *herrlich*, suggesting power.

90. Nietzsche's conception of the great affirmation of life in its eternal recurrence, culminating in the conclusion to Book III of Zarathustra, was evidently suggested by a passage in Schopenhauer (*WWV*, 1.54.372-73): "A man whose senses have become fully permeated with the above-mentioned truths, but who has not yet arrived, by his own experience or further insight, at the recognition that lasting suffering is the essence of

life; who finds life satisfying and is entirely comfortable in it; and who, upon calm reflection, would wish the course of life as he has known it to continue and be repeated forever; whose joy in life is such, in other words, that he would readily and gladly pay for the delights of life with all the discomforts and pains to which it is liable; such a man, I say, stands so "firmly and vigorously upon our well-founded, enduring earth" [Goethe, "Grenzen der Menschheit" (1813)] that he has nothing to fear. Armed with understanding, he will look calmly upon death as it rushes towards him on the wings of time, viewing it as no more than an illusion, an impotent specter that can scare only the weak and that can have no power over anyone who knows that he is himself the will whose image or objectification is the world; who is assured of life and of being ever-present and cannot therefore be frightened by an eternal past or future in which he does not exist, because he recognizes such visions to be merely the vain web of Maya's deceptions; and who thus need fear death as little as the sun need fear the night. Such is the perspective of Arjuna in the *Bhagavad Gita*; such is that of Goethe's Prometheus; and such is also the perspective to which the philosophies of Bruno and Spinoza might lead anyone who will not let himself be dissuaded by the errors and imperfections in their systems."

91. Meant to convey not just obscurity (see par. 2 {339}), but also embarrassment, in reference to the history of the papacy around the 10th century, for instance.

92. With the unification of Germany in 1871.

93. G: *Spaß- und Afterphilosophie.*

94. Friedrich Harms (1819-1880) and Jürgen Bona-Meyer (1829-97), professors of philosophy at the Universities of Berlin and Bonn, respectively, had angered Nietzsche with a political statement that he found so egregiously "stupid" that he thought their universities should have "protested against such an aberration" (*Kommentar*. KSA 14.77). The "pseudo-philosopher

Bona-Meyer" (a polite translation of *Afterphilosoph*) had already appalled Nietzsche with his smug pretention to having demolished Schopenhauer's pessimism (*Nachlaß*: 7.481 [19 [201]]). Harms was close to Fichte, whom Nietzsche despised utterly, and Moritz Carrière (1817-95), at the University of Munich, made for an irresistible target not only because of his name (Professor Career), but also because he had been included, alongside Fichte, in a list of five prominent thinkers who were taken to represent German tradition as a "people of thinkers." Nietzsche derided these five as the leading lights of a mere "thought-shop" (*Denkwirtschaft*): "It would be so edifying to know that we Germans have a wise man here, a wise man there, and so also in Munich. But the nomination of Carrière, the inventor of real idealism and wooden iron, must fill us with particular displeasure. If he possessed even a smattering of wisdom, we would gladly take him for the real thing. What a disgrace it is that our nation does not even have a single wise man, but only five thought-peddlers." (*Nachlaß*: 7.738 [30(16)] and 7.739-40 [30(20)])

95. An alloy of copper and zinc used as a substitute for gold in cheap jewelry.

96. G: *Beschaulichkeit*.

97. One cannot help being reminded of the unceasing upheavals of social conditions, the endless insecurity and agitation that characterizes the bourgeois epoch according to Marx (Part I of the *Communist Manifesto*): "All fixed and encrusted relations with their train of venerable ideas and opinions are undone, and all newly emerging relations become outdated before they get a chance to ossify. All that is traditional and established dissolves into thin air, all that is sacred is profaned, and men are at last compelled to make a sober assessment of their situation in life and their mutual relations."

98. Nietzsche writes *gebildet*, but his point is precisely that these strata are not educated in any meaningful sense (see the

next two sentences), but that their years of schooling merely serve to set them apart and make them *contemptuous* of others. That the spectacle is at the same time *contemptible* is clearly implied.

99. In Act 2, Scene 4 of Wagner's opera, the knight Biterolf challenges Tannhäuser to a duel, to which the latter replies: "You foolish braggart, Biterolf! ... What delights have you poor wretch ever enjoyed? There has been no love to boast of in your life, and the pleasure you have given is hardly worth coming to blows over."

100. The lone wanderer is one of Nietzsche's images for the philosopher. Thus in section 7 {406}: "A true artist, and even more a true philosopher, will often seem to have arisen *by chance* in his times, as a recluse or a lone, left-behind wanderer."

101. *Knirschen* is a crunching or grinding sound such as gravel or ice might make beneath the wanderer's boots, but it is also used more figuratively for gnashing one's teeth and for feeling guilty or remorseful (*zerknirscht*). Thus Zarathustra: "[A] mountain path crunched under the defiance of my foot. Striding silently over the mocking clatter of pebbles, crushing the rock that made it slip, my foot forced its way upward." (Kaufmann III.156; KSA 4.198)

102. Nietzsche may be thinking of Jesus instructing his followers to render unto Caesar what is Caesar's (Matt. 22:21), that is, of his decision to limit the domain subject to religious authority and not to challenge the state head-on. The classic treatment of such realms, both Christian and Protestant, is Luther's essay on "The Freedom of a Christian."

103. Thus Mussolini's summary of fascism: "All within the state, nothing outside the state, nothing against the state."

104. Another echo of Marx, who held that the bourgeoisie would over time compel all nations and peoples to follow its example and become bourgeois themselves: "In a word, the bourgeoisie recreates the world in its own image." (*Communist*

Manifesto, Part I)

105. G: *das Menschliche.*

106. *Menschlichkeit* resonates with a kind of pathos in German that the English *humanity* does not convey.

107. Typhos was considered the deadliest of all monsters in Greek mythology. Zeus banished him beneath Mount Aetna after the most fearsome showdown, and the most disruptive volcanic forces were attributed to his power.

108. Epicurus (341-270 BC) taught that if there are gods, they do not concern themselves much with human affairs and that they neither reward nor rescue, nor punish human beings.

109. Mephistopheles. Nietzsche is playing with the term "demonic," both as a deliberate provocation and with a nod in the direction of the original meaning ("inspired, of supernatural genius or impulses" [*Concise OED*, 2nd edition]) that goes back to at least Socrates invocation of his daemon in Plato's *Apology* (40a-c). In Goethe's play, Mephistopheles introduces himself as "the spirit that forever negates, and rightly so, for all that arises deserves to perish."

110. Faust's thrill-chasing with Mephistopheles as his tour-guide becomes ever more frantic and fantastic in the second part of the tragedy, in which he marries Helen of Troy, among other things.

111. As in the myth of Icaros.

112. A radical, violent revolutionary in the mold of Lucius Sergius Catilina, or Catiline (108 – 62 BC), who plotted against the Roman Republic (Catilinian Conspiracy).

113. Nietzsche takes these lines from book VIII, chapter 5, of *Wilhelm Meisters Lehrjahre*, and plays on the ambiguity in the German word *böse*, which could mean either angry or wicked. Compare also *Zarathustra*: "What matters my virtue? As yet it has not made me rage. How weary I am of my good and my evil!" (Kaufmann I.14; KSA 4.15-16)

114. Faust makes this pronouncement in the first scene in the

study, when he has just summoned Mephistopheles. Unlike the incensed burghers that Nietzsche is imagining, Faust is expressing disdain for the sterility of Mephistopheles' powers, rather than any outrage at evil. He continues: "Shake your fist all you want, it is in vain. Try starting something of your own for a change, you strange son of chaos."

115. Another nod at the lines with which Mephistopheles introduces himself in Goethe's Faust (see footnote above).

116. The German mystic Eckhart von Hochheim, or Meister Eckart (c. 1260 – c. 1327), has been especially admired since it has become a compliment to associate a thinker with the traditions of the East. Schopenhauer declares in ch. 48 (vol. 2) of his *World as Will and Representation* that "at bottom the Buddha and Meister Eckhart taught the same thing; only the former was free to express himself openly, while the latter was forced to cloak his ideas in the garb of Christian myth." Eckart's 52nd German Sermon ("Blessed Are the Poor") is especially remarkable: "I beg of God that I may become detached from God and that I may grasp the truth and enjoy eternity where the highest angels and the lowliest mosquito and the soul are all one — where I once stood and wanted what I was, and was what I wanted... Within the soul there is the One, the source of all insight and love, ... and only he who comes to know this One understands what blessedness is. He no longer recognizes any before or after, nor does he expect to be supplemented by anything arbitrary and external, for he no longer has anything to gain or to lose... It is here that man attains eternal Being — that which he once was, what he is now, and what he will always be."

117. Compare *WWV*, 2.49.737: "There is only *one* error that we are born with: the belief that we exist to be happy."

118. Nietzsche uses the word *Lebenslauf*, or curriculum vitae, playing on the literal meaning: the run of one's life.

119. In Gozzi's comedy "Il re corvo" (1762), Prince Deramo

is not turned to stone, but into a stag, though perhaps an especially dignified one.

120. A rather unorthodox understanding of Nirvana, to say the least.

121. See par. 20 {359}.

122. See par. 4 {340}.

123. See par. 12 {349}. Also *Zarathustra*: "Verily, you could wear no better masks, you men of today, than your own faces!" (Kaufmann II.119; KSA 4.153)

124. An interesting parallel with Ayya Khema's meditations on the Buddhist path: "[L]ife is nothing but an adult education class. If we don't pass the subjects, we just have to sit the examination again. Whatever lesson we have missed, we'll get it again." (*Being Nobody, Going Nowhere* [Boston: Wisdom Publications, 1987], p. 148, also p. 32)

125. Like the German *Zerstreuung*, a common word for amusement or entertainment, distraction is literally a drawing-apart or scattering (from L *trahere*).

126. G: *im Unvergänglichen*. A statement that could have been taken verbatim from Eckart Tolle's books, *The Power of Now* and *A New Earth*, as could much else in this section. Thus also Meister Eckart in his 52nd German Sermon: "By my true nature, which is eternal, I am my own origin, though not by my becoming, which is lost to time." Such pronouncements cannot be understood intellectually, Eckhart warns at the outset and the conclusion of his sermon, but only by those who are equal to them in their very being.

127. That happiness has a way of eluding those who chase after it is a piece of wisdom one encounters in folk-sayings, in quotations from Erasmus to Brecht, and even in academic moral philosophy, say in discussions of utilitarianism. Zen Buddhism stresses especially that whatever is pursued with the idea of gain, however good and important it may be, cannot bear real fruit. (See Suzuki, pp. 57 and 89.) It defines grace,

perhaps the greatest happiness of all, that by most accounts it cannot be earned at all.

128. Nietzsche plays on the fact that *Ent-täuschung* (disappointment) can be literally read to mean un-deceiving, just as disillusionment could be taken as a welcome liberation from illusions.

129. See pars. 37a-b {380-81}.

130. Literally, to put him outside of himself (also in the next sentence).

131. From *Wilhelm Meisters Lehrjahre*, Book VI ("Bekenntnisse einer schönen Seele").

132. It is a central feature of Nietzsche's thought that to be favored (by nature) is to be subject to especially arduous duties. Thus section 8 {412}: "An ordinary earthling may feel inclined to resent those who are more favored than he. May God protect him from receiving their favors himself! For to be so favored means to be put under terrible obligations: the freedom and loneliness of the favored would quickly destroy the ordinary man."

133. Not just any man, but the man who can redeem her.

134. See pars. 4a {340} and 31f {375}.

135. A reference to Argus, a hundred-eyed giant in Greek mythology who is employed by Hera to keep an eye on Io. In Ovid's telling, the memory of his many eyes was preserved in the tail of the peacock.

136. Words spoken without love, as in 1 Cor. 13:1.

137. A central axiom among the ancient Greeks that was given renewed prominence in its Latin version (*Natura non facit saltus*) by the Swedish natural scientist Carl von Linné in his *Philosophia Botanica* (1751).

138. G: *die grosse Aufklärung über das Dasein.*

139. See par. 31g {375}. The reddish light of the early morning was an important image for Nietzsche and his 1881 book *Morgenröte*, known to English readers as *The Dawn* or *Daybreak*,

is literally entitled "The Red of Morning."

140. Goethe made the comment in a letter to Charlotte von Stein (3 March 1785). It was an expression of frustration as much as haughtiness at a time when his artistic aspirations were competing with increasingly tedious worldly responsibilities.

141. In sections 7 and 8, Nietzsche admires Schopenhauer's "free and rugged masculinity" {408, 411} and expresses some concerns over manliness and emasculation {416, 427}. In the text above, however, the emphasis is on human beings in general.

142. Knowing when to stop was never one of Nietzsche's strengths and he continues his Third Meditation for three more sections that spoil the effect of his essay with materials that are much more time-bound and unavailing than what I have translated. So I propose to honor Nietzsche's genius by leaving them out.

Made in the USA
San Bernardino, CA
02 November 2015